British History in Perspective
General Editor: Jeremy Black

PUBLISHED TITLES

Rodney Barker *Politics, Peoples and Government*
C. J. Bartlett *British Foreign Policy in the Twentieth Century*
Jeremy Black *Robert Walpole and the Nature of Politics
in Early Eighteenth-Century Britain*
Anne Curry *The Hundred Years War*
John W. Derry *British Politics in the Age of Fox, Pitt and Liverpool*
William Gibson *Church, State and Society, 1760–1850*
Brian Golding *Conquest and Colonisation: the Normans
in Britain, 1066–1100*
S. J. Gunn *Early Tudor Government, 1485–1558*
Richard Harding *The Evolution of the Sailing Navy, 1509–1815*
Ann Hughes *The Causes of the English Civil War*
Ronald Hutton *The British Republic, 1649–1660*
Kevin Jefferys *The Labour Party since 1945*
D. M. Loades *The Mid-Tudor Crisis, 1545–1565*
Diarmaid MacCulloch *The Later Reformation in England, 1547–1603*
Keith Perry *British Politics and the American Revolution*
A. J. Pollard *The Wars of the Roses*
David Powell *British Politics and the Labour Question, 1868–1990*
Michael Prestwich *English Politics in the Thirteenth Century*
Richard Rex *Henry VIII and the English Reformation*
G. R. Searle *The Liberal Party: Triumph and Disintegration, 1886–1929*
Paul Seaward *The Restoration, 1660–1668*
Robert Stewart *Party and Politics, 1830–1852*
John W. Young *Britain and European Unity, 1945–92*

History of Ireland

D. G. Boyce *The Irish Question and British Politics, 1868–1986*

History of Scotland

Keith M. Brown *Kingdom or Province? Scotland and the Regal Union,
1603–1715*

History of Wales

A. D. Carr *Medieval Wales*
J. Gwynfor Jones *Early Modern Wales, c.1525–1640*

Please see overleaf for forthcoming titles

FORTHCOMING TITLES

John Belcham *Nineteenth-Century Radicalism*
Eugenio Biagini *Gladstone*
Peter Catterall *The Labour Party, 1918–1940*
Gregory Claeys *The French Revolution Debate in Britain*
Pauline Croft *James I*
Eveline Cruickshanks *The Glorious Revolution*
John Davis *British Politics, 1885–1931*
David Dean *Parliament and Politics in Elizabethan and Jacobean England, 1558–1614*
Susan Doran *English Foreign Policy in the Sixteenth Century*
David Eastwood *England, 1750–1850: Government and Community in the Provinces*
Colin Eldridge *The Victorians Overseas*
S. Fielding *Britain and the Impact of World War II*
Angus Hawkins *British Party Politics, 1852–1886*
H. S. Jones *Political Thought in Nineteenth-Century Britain*
D. E. Kennedy *The English Revolution, 1642–1649*
Anthony Milton *Church and Religion in England, 1603–1642*
R. C. Nash *English Foreign Trade and the World Economy, 1600–1800*
W. M. Ormrod *Political Life in England, 1300–1450*
Richard Ovendale *Anglo-American Relations in the Twentieth Century*
David Powell *The Edwardian Crisis: Britain, 1901–1914*
Robin Prior and Trevor Wilson *Britain and the Impact of World War I*
Brian Quintrell *Government and Politics in Early Stuart England*
Stephen Roberts *Governance in England and Wales, 1603–1688*
W. Stafford *John Stuart Mill*
Alan Sykes *The Radical Right in Britain*
Ann Williams *Kingship and Government in Pre-Conquest England*
Michael Young *Charles I*

History of Ireland

Toby Barnard *The Kingdom of Ireland, 1641–1740*
Sean Duffy *Ireland in the Middle Ages*
Alan Heesom *The Anglo-Irish Union, 1800–1922*
Hiram Morgan *Ireland in the Early Modern Periphery, 1534–1690*

History of Scotland

I. G. C. Hutchinson *Scottish Politics in the Twentieth Century*
Roger Mason *Kingship and Tyranny? Scotland, 1513–1603*
John McCaffrey *Scotland in the Nineteenth Century*
John Shaw *The Political History of Eighteenth-Century Scotland*
Bruce Webster *Scotland in the Middle Ages*

History of Wales

Gareth Jones *Wales, 1700–1980: Crisis of Identity*

MEDIEVAL WALES

A. D. CARR

St. Martin's Press

First published in Great Britain 1995 by
MACMILLAN PRESS LTD
Houndmills, Basingstoke, Hampshire RG21 2XS
and London
Companies and representatives
throughout the world

A catalogue record for this book is available
from the British Library.

ISBN 0–333–54772–1 hardcover
ISBN 0–333–54773–X paperback

10   9   8   7   6   5   4   3   2   1
04 03 02 01 00 99 98 97 96 95

Printed in Malaysia

First published in the United States of America 1995 by
Scholarly and Reference Division,
ST. MARTIN'S PRESS, INC.,
175 Fifth Avenue,
New York, N.Y. 10010

ISBN 0–312–12509–7

Library of Congress Cataloging-in-Publication Data
Carr, A. D. (Anthony D.), 1938–
Medieval Wales / A. D. Carr.
p.   cm. — (British history in perspective)
Includes bibliographical references (p.   ) and index.
ISBN 0–312–12509–7
1. Wales—History—1063–1536.   I. Title.   II. Series: British
history in perspective (Houndmills, Basingstoke, England).
DA715.C37   1995
942.9'03—dc20
                                        94–38197
                                        CIP

For my mother and in memory of my father

CONTENTS

Contents

PREFACE

In this book I have tried to examine the main features of the history of Wales between the death of Gruffydd ap Llywelyn in 1064 on the eve of the coming of the Normans and the execution of the last marcher magnate, Edward Stafford, duke of Buckingham, in 1521, in many ways a more appropriate date than 1536 to mark the end of the middle ages. It is the fruit of a process of reading, of research, of conversations with colleagues and friends, of teaching and of thinking over a number of years, and the bibliography and footnotes reflect more debts than can be enumerated here; its shortcomings are all my own work. I am indebted to my publishing editor, Vanessa Graham, and to Keith Povey, editorial services consultant, for their advice and assistance in guiding the book through the press. Above all, I am grateful to my wife Glenda for her patience and forbearance, especially in reading the entire work, and for so many suggestions which have added to the clarity of the original.

A. D. Carr

GLOSSARY

bastide	A planned fortified town of the kind established in Gascony by John, Henry III and Edward I; the term is often applied to Edward's castle boroughs in north Wales.
cantref	The basic Welsh territorial administrative unit.
commote	A subdivision of the cantref, usually corresponding in size to the English hundred.
cydfod (pl. *cydfodau*)	A formal agreement, usually between two marcher lordships or between a lordship and the royal authorities, usually for the settlement of disputes or the extradition of criminals.
cymorth	A payment due by tenants to a marcher lord, originally in the form of cattle.
distain	The steward or seneschal of a Welsh ruler; in thirteenth-century Gwynedd the prince's chief adviser.
gafael	A holding of land held by a kindred group. In some parts of Wales it was the predominant unit of tenure, in others it was a subdivision of the *gwely* (q.v.).

galanas Compensation for homicide payable by the kindred of the killer to the kindred of the victim under Welsh law and the procedure for payment.

gwely A free kindred group, descended from a common ancestor and sharing proprietary rights in land, also the actual land held by the group.

penteulu The commander of a Welsh ruler's household troops, usually a close relative.

taeog A bondman or unfree tenant, corresponding to the English villein.

teulu The household troops or warband of a Welsh ruler.

tir cyfrif The most onerous form of unfree tenure. A township or community of this nature owed a fixed burden of rents and services shared equally among all adult males; if there were only one there, he owed it all.

tir gwelyog A tenure under which an unfree kindred group held land in *gwelyau*. Although unfree, such tenants had a heritable interest.

tir prid A form of gage used extensively in medieval Wales to circumvent the prohibition of alienation of hereditary land. Land was initially pledged for a term of four years; if it were not redeemed at the end of this term, the pledge was renewed for a further term and this could continue indefinitely.

uchelwr
(pl. *uchelwyr*)

The term generally used for the land-owning class. It originally meant any free-born Welsh-man, but it later came to apply to those families of good descent who were the traditional leaders of their communities and the patrons of the poets.

MAPS

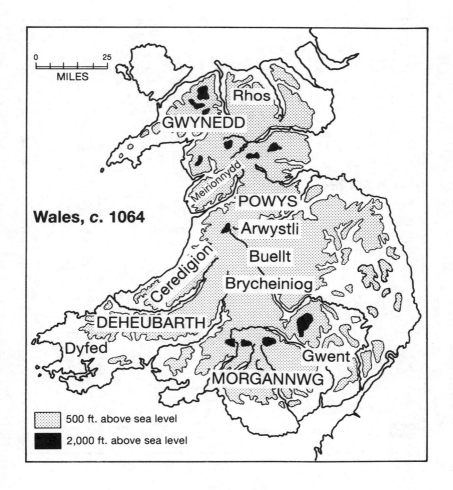

0   25
MILES

Rhos

GWYNEDD

Meirionnydd

POWYS

Wales, *c.* 1064

Arwystli

Ceredigion

Buellt

Brycheiniog

DEHEUBARTH

Dyfed

Gwent

MORGANNWG

- 500 ft. above sea level
- 2,000 ft. above sea level

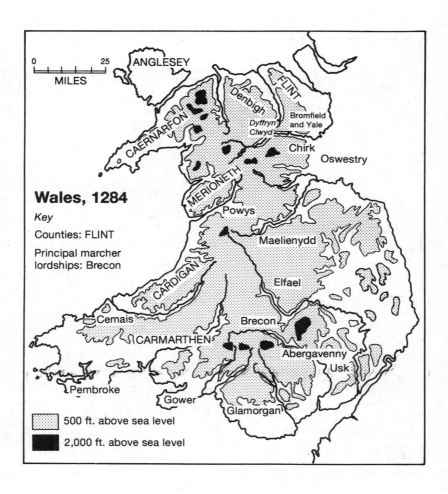

Wales, 1284

Key

Counties: FLINT

Principal marcher
lordships: Brecon

ANGLESEY

FLINT

Denbigh

Bromfield
and Yale

*Dyffryn
Clwyd*

Chirk

CAERNARFON

Oswestry

MERIONETH

Powys

Maelienydd

CARDIGAN

Elfael

Cemais

CARMARTHEN

Brecon

Abergavenny

Usk

Pembroke

Gower

Glamorgan

0   25
MILES

500 ft. above sea level

2,000 ft. above sea level

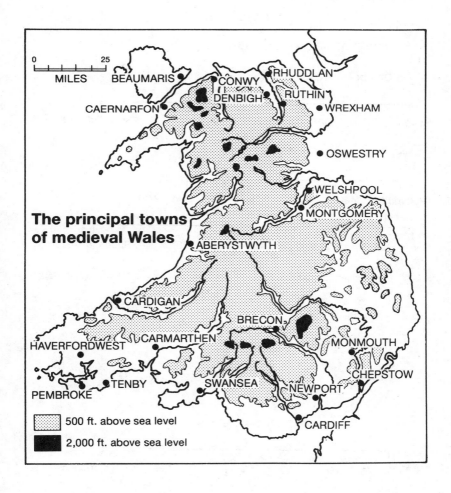

The principal towns of medieval Wales

0 MILES 25

BEAUMARIS
CAERNARFON
CONWY
RHUDDLAN
DENBIGH
RUTHIN
WREXHAM
OSWESTRY
WELSHPOOL
MONTGOMERY
ABERYSTWYTH
CARDIGAN
BRECON
CARMARTHEN
MONMOUTH
HAVERFORDWEST
CHEPSTOW
TENBY
SWANSEA
NEWPORT
PEMBROKE
CARDIFF

500 ft. above sea level
2,000 ft. above sea level

GENEALOGICAL TABLES

Gwynedd

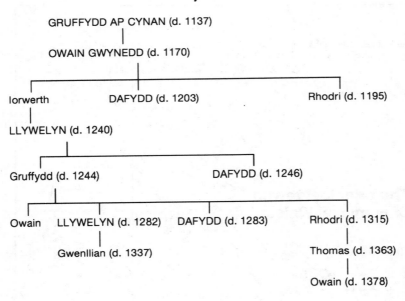

GRUFFYDD AP CYNAN (d. 1137)

OWAIN GWYNEDD (d. 1170)

Iorwerth — DAFYDD (d. 1203) — Rhodri (d. 1195)

LLYWELYN (d. 1240)

Gruffydd (d. 1244) — DAFYDD (d. 1246)

Owain — LLYWELYN (d. 1282) — DAFYDD (d. 1283) — Rhodri (d. 1315)

Gwenllian (d. 1337)

Thomas (d. 1363)

Owain (d. 1378)

Deheubarth

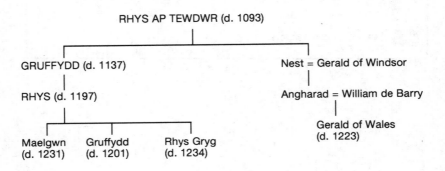

RHYS AP TEWDWR (d. 1093)

GRUFFYDD (d. 1137) — Nest = Gerald of Windsor

RHYS (d. 1197) — Angharad = William de Barry

Maelgwn (d. 1231) — Gruffydd (d. 1201) — Rhys Gryg (d. 1234)

Gerald of Wales (d. 1223)

Powys

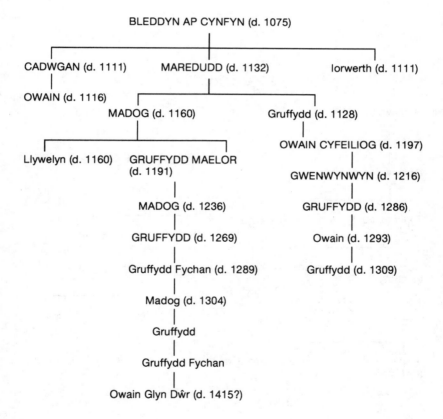

BLEDDYN AP CYNFYN (d. 1075)

CADWGAN (d. 1111)   MAREDUDD (d. 1132)   Iorwerth (d. 1111)

OWAIN (d. 1116)

MADOG (d. 1160)   Gruffydd (d. 1128)

Llywelyn (d. 1160)   GRUFFYDD MAELOR (d. 1191)   OWAIN CYFEILIOG (d. 1197)

GWENWYNWYN (d. 1216)

MADOG (d. 1236)   GRUFFYDD (d. 1286)

GRUFFYDD (d. 1269)   Owain (d. 1293)

Gruffydd Fychan (d. 1289)   Gruffydd (d. 1309)

Madog (d. 1304)

Gruffydd

Gruffydd Fychan

Owain Glyn Dŵr (d. 1415?)

The Tudor Lineage

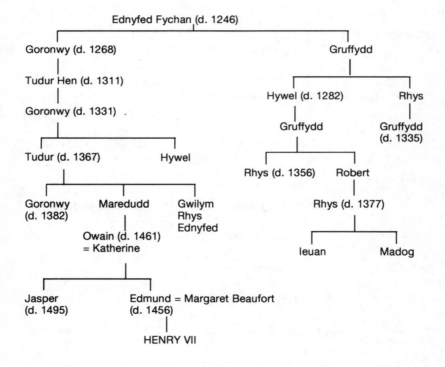

INTRODUCTION

For a long time, as one leading Welsh historian has said, the study of the history of Wales was 'marginalized . . . even within Wales itself'.[1] In some historical quarters its practitioners were often looked on with a kind of amused tolerance and a feeling that they ought to have been able to find something more useful to do. What awareness there was of Welsh history tended to be composed of stereotypes, ranging from fiercely-moustached medieval tribal chieftains to Mam scrubbing the doorstep in Llwynypia, while her menfolk sang hymns in four-part harmony as the cage descended the shaft. Various reasons can be suggested for this; the fact that political independence came to an end in 1282–3, so that the Welsh nation was never able to develop into a state, may have conditioned the view of some commentators, while British history has, until recently, been an essentially London-based history, its chronological bench-marks being largely associated with events in the history of England. This has been particularly true of the history of medieval Wales, often relegated to a series of footnotes. Welsh appearances in the historical record have usually been connected with Norman invasions and the creation of the march, with Edward I's conquest, with the revolt of Owain Glyn Dŵr (usually described as Owen Glendower) and with Henry Tudor's march to Bosworth; Henry's descent from Ednyfed Fychan is sometimes mentioned, but without any further details. A favourite adjective when referring to the medieval Welsh social and political

1

structure was 'tribal', particularly in connection with any discussion of medieval Welsh law, a law which Archbishop Pecham of Canterbury in 1282 claimed came from the devil.[2] There have been exceptions and there is by now an awareness of recent scholarship; some Welsh historians have reached the commanding heights of the British historical profession and in doing so have emphasised the importance and relevance of their own specialist studies, but on the whole Welsh history, and particularly medieval Welsh history, has in the past received little attention in its own right outside Wales.

The position within Wales was not much better. The framers of examination syllabuses strove gallantly to ensure a place for Welsh history in the curriculum, but teaching in Welsh schools concentrated on the history of England. As far as the middle ages were concerned, the two Llywelyns and Owain Glyn Dŵr were viewed in the distorting mirror of nineteenth-century national consciousness as patriotic heroes. Wales as a whole was less aware of its history than Scotland or Ireland; on the one hand it has sometimes been argued that a distinct identity did not emerge until the coming of large-scale industrialisation and the social consequences which flowed from it, and on the other medieval Wales was sometimes seen through a romantic haze as a world of aristocratic values and a hierarchic and ordered society in an appeal to history which owed more to the reading of contemporary poetry than to a rigorous historical analysis.[3]

But the twentieth century, and particularly the past thirty years, has seen an upsurge in Welsh historical studies and the transformation of our understanding of medieval Wales is described in the first chapter of this book. The simplicities of the past have been replaced by an appreciation of the complexities of what was, when the Normans first came, a political system rather than a political unit. A succession of studies has shed light on the nature of political authority, both Welsh and Anglo-Norman, on the gradual polarisation of that authority in native Wales, on the efforts of thirteenth-century princes to create a Welsh polity and on the causes of the final loss of independence. The period after the conquest has also been opened up and there is a clearer perception of the causes, political, social and economic, of the revolt of Owain Glyn Dŵr and of the nature and structure of late medieval society. This is no longer a world of unsophisticated princes in a constant state of war with England or with each other, of the division of kingdoms on the deaths of rulers or, after 1282, of crude oppression and exploitation by alien officials; post-conquest Wales, in particular, is now seen as an environment in which the traditional leaders of local communities in both principality and march exercised and retained that power and influence which were to survive far beyond the end of the middle ages. Much of the history of medieval Wales is concerned with the impact of forces which affected most of western Europe; these include the advent of the Normans, the new political and legal influences in the thirteenth century, the Black Death, and late medieval popular rebellion, but all of these had a Welsh dimension. The sources available to the historian of medieval Wales are by no means as rich as those available to his or her English counterpart, but this is true of most European nations as far as the middle ages are concerned; the ones that do exist are far from exhausted.

There is also a greater understanding of the importance of the study of the history of medieval Wales. For the Welsh historian it is an essential part of the comprehension of the development of Welsh identity and nationhood; for the historian of the British Isles it is an integral part of the prehistory of the multi-national British state and a reminder that the component nations of that state all have their own distinct histories and identities. This book is an attempt to outline and clarify the main strands in the history of medieval Wales; it does not claim in any way to be an exhaustive account, but it may help to explain the continued presence of a separate nation with its own language, culture and identity to the west of Offa's Dyke.

1

OF HISTORY AND HISTORIANS

The Medieval View

Medieval Welshmen had a very clear perception of their history. Their understanding of it stemmed from one seminal work, Geoffrey of Monmouth's *Historia Regum Britanniae*, completed about 1136, which forms the basis of the Matter of Britain, one of the three great collections. of stories of heroes from medieval Europe. Geoffrey set out to write the history of the Britons from the arrival of Brutus, a refugee from the fall of Troy who gave his name to Britain, to the death of the Welsh king Cadwaladr in 688; he claimed that his *History* was a Latin translation of a 'very old book in the British tongue'.[1] In it is recounted the legendary history of Britain and its kings, above all of Arthur, and also of the magician and prophet Merlin; indeed, Geoffrey was the conduit through which the whole Arthurian corpus found its way to Europe to become a part of the western cultural tradition. But for the Welsh Geoffrey provided an explanation of who they were and whence they had come. The story of their Trojan descent gave them a link with the world of classical antiquity, especially Rome, since Brutus was said to have been a descendant of Aeneas. This link had always been important; the Roman presence in Wales had cast a long shadow and for several centuries after the departure of the legions Rome was seen as the fount of all legitimate authority. At the end of the *Historia* an

4

angelic voice declares that the Britons will not rule again in Britain until some time in the future; this provided a note of hope after the conquest of 1282 and contributed to that vein of prophecy which was to come to the surface on several occasions in late medieval Wales.[2] Geoffrey's influence on Welsh historical thinking was profound and long-lived; the *Historia* was translated into Welsh under the title *Brut y Brenhinedd* more than once and the very word *Brut*, meaning a history or a chronicle, derives from the eponymous Trojan. One commentator has described it as 'granting the Welsh their first coherent history of themselves, a glorious view of their past', and the influence of Geoffrey on Welsh historiography, with the accompanying faith in his account, survived until the eighteenth century and later.[3]

The *Historia Regum Britanniae* provided medieval Wales with its vision of its past and it lies at the root of the main source for Welsh history before the conquest. England is rich in twelfth- and thirteenth-century chronicles but Wales can boast no such wealth; the principal piece of medieval Welsh historical writing is *Brut y Tywysogyon* or *The Chronicle of the Princes*. This is a conscious literary compilation, being a Welsh translation of a Latin original, now lost, written near the end of the thirteenth century, probably at the Cistercian abbey of Strata Florida in Cardiganshire.[4] In a sense it is a continuation of the *Historia*, beginning where Geoffrey left off, and it may have been intended by its author as a kind of elegy on the age of the princes. It seems in large part to be based on a set of annals, kept in the thirteenth century at Strata Florida and before that at Llanbadarn Fawr near Aberystwyth and St David's, and the author may have drawn on other sources. Some of these have survived; *Annales Cambriae* is a set of Latin annals which begins very early and runs on into the thirteenth century and the *Cronica de Wallia*, contained in a manuscript in Exeter Cathedral Library, covers the period from 1190 to 1266.[5] These sources, of course, have their limitations which reflect their provenance and the circumstances of their composition. *Brut y Tywysogyon* itself, being probably associated with Strata Florida, has far more to say about Deheubarth and its rulers than about Gwynedd or Powys.

There is, for example, virtually nothing about the long-drawn-out struggle for the control of Gwynedd between 1170 and 1200, or about the consequent rise to power of Llywelyn ab Iorwerth, surely a worthy theme for the historian of the Welsh princes. The surviving contributory texts are of Deheubarth provenance and this may suggest that the Gwynedd and Powys references were drawn from annals, now lost, from those two kingdoms.

There is some evidence which points to an independent tradition of historical writing in Gwynedd. There is, for example, the tract *O Oes Gwrtheyrn Gwrtheneu* (*From the Age of Vortigern*) which is a series of chronological notes recording the intervals between events; almost all these events are to do with Gwynedd and some do not appear in any other source.[6] There also survives a biography of Gruffydd ap Cynan, again a Welsh translation of a Latin original; this likewise mentions historical episodes not recorded in *Brut y Tywysogyon* and may, therefore, draw on a separate Gwynedd historiographical tradition which one would expect to have persisted.[7] This is the only surviving medieval Welsh secular biography, but at the end of the seventeenth century the Welsh scholar Edward Lhwyd referred in a letter to a life of Llywelyn ab Iorwerth and his son Dafydd ap Llywelyn, known to the antiquary Robert Vaughan, which had been among the manuscripts of Benet (now Corpus Christi) College, Cambridge; the manuscript cannot now be traced.[8] Wales produced no William of Malmesbury or Matthew Paris, but enough survives to show that there was a tradition of historical writing in Wales and also what contemporaries saw as a coherent theme; there are several examples of Dares Phrygius's *History of Troy*, the *Historia Regum* and *Brut y Tywysogyon* bound together in a single volume and this represents this coherence.[9] Some English writers, particularly Matthew Paris, do describe events in Wales, often those which go unrecorded in the *Brut* (an example is Matthew's reference to Llywelyn ab Iorwerth's stroke in 1237), but the *Brut* offers a Welsh view of Welsh events.

There is even less Welsh historical writing from the post-conquest period. One text of *Brut y Tywysogyon* goes as far as 1332, but this continuation deals almost entirely with events in north-east Wales, which suggests a connection with the Cistercian abbey of Valle Crucis. The chronicle of Adam of Usk, himself a Welshman, does give some information about the Glyn Dŵr revolt and there are one or two small chronicles.[10] But perhaps the most interesting piece of historical writing about the revolt is a pamphlet, *Hanes Owain Glandwr* [sic], *blaenor y Cymry mewn rhyfel* (*The History of Owain Glyn Dŵr, leader of the Welsh in war*), published at Caernarfon in 1833 and written by a self-educated antiquary, William Owen.[11] This pamphlet contains information about the revolt which is not available elsewhere and which has the stamp of authenticity. Owen claimed that he had used a history of the revolt written in Welsh by a Beaumaris physician, David Bulkeley, in 1520, which was in his possession, but which has not been seen since.

Reformation and Renaissance

Both Reformation and Renaissance had a significant impact on Welsh historical writing and thinking. The Reformation involved an appeal to history and in Wales this meant the *Historia Regum*. According to this, Christianity came to Britain in the second century when the British king Lucius asked Pope Eleutherius to send missionaries; the story had earlier been cited by the chapter of St David's cathedral when, in the twelfth century, it claimed metropolitan status for the see.[12] This view of the origins of British Christianity was set out by Richard Davies, bishop of St David's, in his *Epistol at y Cembru* (*Epistle to the Welsh*) which formed the preface to the first Welsh translation of the New Testament in 1567.[13] The purpose of Davies's *Epistle* was to make the Reformation acceptable to the Welsh people and to convince them that Protestantism was not a new English import. The original British church had been apostolic and doctrinally pure, but in 597 Augustine had come from Rome and had brought with him all kinds of bad ecclesiastical practices, thereby leading the church in Britain astray. The purpose of the Reformation had been to restore the usages of the primitive

British church and to sweep away all the Roman accretions. The Reformation was not a revolution; it was a return to a primitive apostolic Christianity. Richard Davies was therefore responsible, at least in part, for the myth of a Celtic church which was something apart from Rome, a myth which dies very hard.[14]

But it was the Renaissance which had the greater influence on the Welsh historiographical tradition. Wales was the only Celtic country to experience the impact of the new learning on its language and culture in which the young humanists emerging from the universities took immense pride. Welsh self-confidence had also been boosted by Henry Tudor's victory at Bosworth and the consequent feeling that the prophecies had been fulfilled. There was, too, the negative impact of the new humanist influence. The *Historia Regum* was generally accepted in both Wales and England as the authentic account of British historical origins, but in 1534 there was published the *Anglica Historia* of the Italian humanist Polydore Vergil, who had spent many years in England.[15] In this book Polydore Vergil attacked Geoffrey of Monmouth, accusing him of lying and of overpraising the Britons to such an extent as to make them a laughing-stock. This was nothing new; the twelfth-century historian William of Newburgh had been just as sceptical. But the reaction in Wales and England was one of outrage and many writers in both countries sprang to Geoffrey's defence. One Welsh humanist who did so was the Denbigh physician Humphrey Lhuyd (1527–1568) whose *Commentarioli Britannicae Descriptionis Fragmentum* was published at Cologne in 1572 after his death. Lhuyd defended Geoffrey and attacked Polydore Vergil; his main contribution to the study of medieval Wales, however, was his unpublished translation of *Brut y Tywysogyon*, the earlier part of which he believed was the work of Caradog of Llancarfan. This work was taken up and continued by one of the leading figures of the Renaissance in Wales, Dr David Powel (*c.* 1552–98), the vicar of Ruabon in Denbighshire who in 1584 published *The Historie of Cambria, now called Wales*, the first printed history of Wales.

Powel's *Historie* was, without a doubt, the most important and influential book on the history of Wales to be published before the twentieth century; it is the *fons et origo* of practically everything published on the history of medieval Wales before 1911. He had been asked by Sir Henry Sidney, the President of the Council in the Marches of Wales, whose chaplain he was, to prepare Humphrey Lhuyd's translation of the *Brut* for publication, but the final product was a great deal more. Some of Lhuyd's material did not derive from the *Brut* at all and may have stemmed from independent traditions. This was included by Powel in the *Historie*; here, for example, is the first appearance in print of the story of Edward I presenting his infant son to the Welsh leaders as their new prince and also the story of Madog ab Owain Gwynedd's discovery of America in the twelfth century. The latter was known to Lhuyd and may have originated with the Welsh magus Dr John Dee as a riposte to Spanish claims in the New World by right of discovery.[16] He also drew on English chronicles and may have had access to some of the public records. Like his contemporaries, he defended Geoffrey of Monmouth and he laid great stress on the benefits which the house of Tudor and the Acts of Union had brought to Wales. The *Historie* was reprinted in 1811; in 1697 an adaptation, making use of the papers of the great seventeenth-century antiquary Robert Vaughan of Hengwrt, was produced by William Wynne of Garthewin in Denbighshire. Wynne's book went through several reprints, the last being in 1832.

Writers like Lhuyd and Powel were self-conscious literary artists whose object was to set out the whole history of Wales and to defend the traditional view of it; Lhuyd sought to counter the 'sclandrous lies' of Polydore Vergil, while in his preface Powel wrote that he undertook his work in response to 'the slanderous report of such writers, as in their books do enforce everie thing that is done by the Welshmen to their discredit, leaving out all the causes and circumstances of the same'.[17] The sixteenth century, however, also saw the emergence of another kind of student of the past, who investigated and collected information about it for its own sake; this was the antiquary. The first Welsh antiquaries were probably the Glamorgan squire Sir Edward Stradling, whose account of the Norman conquest of Glamorgan was included by Powel in the *Historie*, and Rice Merrick or Rhys Amheurug of Cottrell in the same county, who completed his *Booke of Glamorganshire Antiquities* in 1575, although it was not published for the first time until 1825. The Pembrokeshire squire George Owen (1552–1613) wrote copiously about the history of his own county and also composed a *Treatise of Lordshipps Marchers in Wales*; he moved in English antiquarian circles and was a friend of William Camden.[18] Another country squire was Sir John Wynn of Gwydir in Caernarfonshire (d. 1627), a man of overweening ambition and arrogance and of little scruple where the interests of himself and his family were concerned, but also a man of some culture. He wrote a history of his family, using original documentary sources; he had access to the archives of the principality of north Wales at Caernarfon, as well as his own family papers.[19] He described the disorder of the fifteenth century and the migration of his ancestor from south Caernarfonshire to the Conwy valley because of endless family feuds. Sir John's object was to glorify his own family; he was responsible for the story that Edward I had ordered the massacre of the bards, a story which almost acquired the status of Holy Writ and which, in the nineteenth century, inspired a Hungarian poet to compose a poem on the subject, as had Thomas Gray earlier.[20] In fact, the story was made up by Sir John to explain the lack of any early poetry to his family, which did not emerge as patrons of the poets until the sixteenth century.

The Eighteenth and Nineteenth Centuries

The eighteenth century saw the continuation of the work of the antiquaries. These were not exclusively Welsh; the first printed text of the Welsh laws, published in 1730, was the work of an English clergyman, William Wotton, and another English scholar, Browne Willis, produced historical surveys of the four Welsh cathedrals between 1717 and 1721. The first half of the century is also associated with the last defender of the Galfridian tradition, Theophilus Evans (1693–1767), who is best

10

remembered for his *Drych y Prif Oesoedd* (*The Mirror of the First Ages*), two editions of which appeared in 1716 and 1740. In terms of language and style this is a classic, but it cannot be considered a serious work of history by modern standards.

Perhaps the most important eighteenth-century contribution to the study of the history of medieval Wales was that of Thomas Pennant (1726–98). Pennant, a Flintshire squire, was a many-sided figure. He was a naturalist who corresponded with many scientists in Britain and abroad and he wrote a historical account of his own neighbourhood, but he is remembered above all as a traveller, and particularly for his *Tours in Wales*, first published between 1778 and 1781. The *Tours* include a great deal of historical material; the most interesting section may be that in which Pennant rehabilitated Owain Glyn Dŵr and, in effect, made him a national hero.[21] Earlier writers had, on the whole, been unsympathetic to Owain; in the sixteenth century it was generally agreed that Wales had attained its manifest destiny at Bosworth and David Powel dismissed his claim to be prince of Wales, although Shakespeare's portrayal of him in *King Henry IV, Part I* is of a cultivated gentleman. But Pennant described his career at some length and saw the revolt as a bid for Welsh freedom and in this he had a profound influence on later writers.

The production of histories of Wales continued in the nineteenth century, with most of them concentrating on the period before 1282 and continuing to be based on the work of David Powel, although Geoffrey of Monmouth had by now been abandoned. One of the best of these histories was the first to be written in Welsh, *Hanes Cymru a Chenedl y Cymry* (*The History of Wales and the Welsh Nation*), published in 1842 by Thomas Price, better known by his bardic name Carnhuanawc, one of the foremost Celtic scholars of his day; other histories to appear during the century included a two-volume work by B. B. Woodward, later librarian at Windsor Castle (1853), and the *History of Wales* by Jane Williams (1869). The tradition established by the antiquaries was also maintained; the first Welsh historical and archaeological journal, *Archaeologia Cambrensis*, first appeared in 1846 and this was followed by the foundation of

11

the Cambrian Archaeological Association a year later. The first county historical society, the Powysland Club, with its journal, *Montgomeryshire Collections*, was founded in 1868. These Welsh county journals have always included articles of more than local importance, many of them being on medieval topics. Most of the original members of these societies came from the ranks of the gentry and the clergy, but during the century the history of Wales was becoming a more popular study, with valuable work being done by self-educated scholars like the Merthyr Tydfil pharmacist Thomas Stephens (1821–75) and the Anglesey weaver Robert John Pryse (Gweirydd ap Rhys, 1807–89); this wider interest may be associated with an increasing national awareness which was becoming more evident as the nineteenth century advanced and which may be discerned in many areas of Welsh life. Significant contributions were also made by such scholars as the engineer G. T. Clark (1809–98) and the industrial chemist A. N. Palmer (1847–1915) who may justly be described as the father of modern Welsh local historical studies.

The great change in the nature of historical scholarship came to Britain in the second half of the nineteenth century, when history became a subject of academic study in the universities; the other contributory factor was the gradual opening of European archives to scholars. Wales had no university; a University of Wales with the power to award its own degrees did not come until 1893. The first historian of medieval Wales to make use of the resources of the Public Record Office was not an academic; he was not even a graduate. Edward Owen (1853–1943) was a civil servant in the India Office who spent all his spare time in the British Museum and the Record Office. Owen contributed many papers to historical journals; his most important piece of work was the long article which he published in 1900 in which he proved that the legendary hero Owain Lawgoch, the mercenary captain in French service 'Yvain de Galles' and the last direct heir of the Gwynedd dynasty assassinated in 1378, Owain ap Thomas ap Rhodri, were one and the same person.[22] Frederic Seebohm's *Tribal System in Wales*, first published in 1895, also made use of material from the public records and contains a valuable appendix of documents. The infrastructure necessary for serious historical research was also developing; the Record Commission, established in 1800, had published some Welsh material, including the texts of the Laws (1841) and the great series of calendars of Chancery enrolments was under way.[23] The Rolls Series included texts of *Brut y Tywysogyon* and *Annales Cambriae*, albeit in very poor and inadequate editions. The Honourable Society of Cymmrodorion embarked on its Record Series in 1893 and the National Library at Aberystwyth was founded in 1907; this was to be followed by other archive repositories and the surviving medieval records of the principality and of some marcher lordships had already been gathered in to the Public Record Office.

The New Welsh History

It was the University of Wales which was to provide the academic framework for the study of the history of Wales and which was to move it forward from its dependence on David Powel. One important influence was that of one of the greatest English medievalists, T. F. Tout, who began his career as Professor of History at St David's College, Lampeter, and who always took an interest in Welsh historical studies thereafter. The initial contribution by the colleges of the University was by individuals; the name which stands out here is that of John Edward Lloyd (1861–1947). Lloyd was a product of that Liverpool–Welsh community which provided north Wales with its only substantial urban middle class. He began his career at Aberystwyth, but in 1892 he moved to Bangor, initially as registrar; in 1895 he began to teach medieval Welsh history and in 1899 he was appointed to the Chair of History. Lloyd's first major article was one on 'Wales and the coming of the Normans', which appeared in 1900; his greatest work, however, was *A History of Wales from the earliest times to the Edwardian Conquest*, which appeared in two volumes in 1911.[24] This may be described as a revolutionary book, not so much because of its insights as because it was the first major book on Welsh history written in accordance with modern standards of historical scholarship; as Tout said in his review of it in the *English Historical Review*, 'a book on such lines of such a type has never previously been written'.[25] This was the first professional critical study of medieval Wales; it provided the basic narrative but it also tried to explain how and why and, as the footnotes reveal, it was rooted in its author's detailed knowledge of the topography of Wales. Later historians have offered new interpretations and Lloyd is no longer the indispensable guide through the tangled thickets of pre-Norman Wales, but as the narrative account of Welsh history between 1063 and 1267 the book has stood the test of time. It also, for the first time, gave Welsh history, historians and historical scholarship authority and credibility in a wider historical world. This was the history of Wales with Wales at the centre of the stage, not as a footnote to what may have been going on in England at any time. Nor should its importance within Wales be discounted; it appeared at a time when national confidence was at its peak and may have made its own contribution. Lloyd showed that Wales had a history like any other nation.

His work is not above criticism. It was based on chronicles and on what pre-1282 public records were available in print, not on archives. It was sometimes suggested that Lloyd had finished in 1282 because subsequent source material had not been printed. He himself half admitted this and it is only fair to add that he came of a generation which tended not to work on original material and which was sometimes inclined to look down on grubbers in the public records.[26] His other major work, *Owen Glendower* (1931), was of the same type; Lloyd aimed to collect all the information available at that time and to reduce it to order. And it was this establishment of order that was, perhaps, his most important achievement; he provided a firm foundation for later interpretation and it is safe to say that the flowering of studies in medieval Welsh history over the past thirty years would not have come about were it not for his efforts. The *History of Wales* and *Owen Glendower* are still required reading; indeed, there has been no detailed general work on the revolt since Lloyd and his contribution to the understanding of medieval Wales is reflected in many articles.

The other founding father of the modern study of medieval Wales, E. A. Lewis (1880–1942), was a very different kind of historian. Lewis was a graduate of the University of Wales; in fact, he was the first graduate of the University to become a professional historian and he spent his entire career at his old college at Aberystwyth. In 1903 he published 'The decay of tribalism in north Wales', a study which was, in its way, as innovative as Lloyd's *History of Wales*.[27] It was an examination, based on the accounts of principality officials in the Public Record Office, of the decline of the Welsh social pattern and the impact of the Black Death in the fourteenth century and it was accompanied by a selection of documents. This was a pioneering piece of work; for the first time a historian had turned his attention to medieval Wales after 1282 and its social and economic history. In 1912 Lewis produced another trail-blazing archive-based study, *The Mediaeval Boroughs of Snowdonia*, which examined the boroughs of north-west Wales, and he also published two substantial articles on trade and industry in late medieval Wales.[28] It was Lewis who showed what could be done with financial documents, the only substantial corpus of medieval principality material to survive among the public records.

Lloyd and Lewis were the pioneers. They founded no school and initiated no debates; their achievement was to begin the serious study of medieval Wales. The next outstanding figure was J. G. Edwards (1891–1976); he and Lloyd were the only Welsh historians to be knighted. Edwards was not a graduate of the University of Wales; he was educated at Oxford and Manchester, where he came under the influence of Tout. From there he returned to Oxford and he ended his career as Director of the University of London Institute of Historical Research. Much of his work was on the history of the medieval English parliament, but he never lost interest in Welsh history and his contributions spanned more than half a century, the first being in 1914 when he was still a research student. It can be said of

J. G. Edwards that each time he wrote on some aspect of the history of Wales new avenues of research were opened up. His 1928 lecture on 'Hywel Dda and the Welsh lawbooks' subjected the prefaces of the lawbooks and the Hywel Dda legend to a devastating critical analysis and although other scholars, including Lloyd, had already made use of the evidence of the laws, the modern study of Welsh law really stems from this lecture.[29] In his introduction to the 1940 edition of *Littere Wallie*, a collection of thirteenth-century documents relating to Anglo-Welsh relations, he provided the first detailed discussion of the events leading up to the final crisis of 1282, explaining what the princes were trying to do and why the conquest happened; again this is the point of departure for all subsequent discussion.[30] His 1944 lecture on 'Edward I's castle-building in Wales' was likewise a seminal work on which his pupil A. J. Taylor was to build and another lecture in 1956, 'The Normans and the Welsh march', examined the origins and the nature of marcher lordship, putting it into its Welsh context.[31] In 1967 he delivered a public lecture at Caernarfon to commemorate the seventh centenary of the Treaty of Montgomery; in this he stressed the continuity of the principality recognised in that year, pointing out that as an institution it survived the events of 1282–3 and continued as a constitutional entity until 1536.[32]

If J. G. Edwards continued the work of Lloyd, the mantle of E. A. Lewis descended on the shoulders of William Rees (1887–1978). A graduate of Cardiff, he was appointed to a post there in 1920 and he remained there until his retirement. As a young man he spent several years in full-time research in the Public Record Office, devoting himself to the mass of account rolls from the southern principality and the march; the fruit of this was *South Wales and the March, 1284–1415*, published in 1924, an immensely detailed study which broke so much new ground that it was not universally well-received by reviewers.[33] He had already produced what is still the only study of the Black Death in Wales (1920) and in 1933 came the *Map of South Wales and the Border in the Fourteenth Century*.[34] This is an astonishing achievement; in our age of collaborative research projects it seems

16

incredible that it could have been produced by one man and it received high praise from no less a historian than Marc Bloch. Rees produced a great deal more, including a *Historical Atlas of Wales* (1951); two of his most substantial pieces of work appeared when he was in his ninth decade.[35]

One of the most significant figures in modern Welsh historiography was T. Jones Pierce (1905–64). Like Lloyd he was a native of Liverpool and it was there that he graduated. On Lloyd's retirement he was appointed a lecturer at Bangor; he moved subsequently to Aberystwyth. Jones Pierce made what can only be described as a revolutionary contribution to medieval Welsh studies. His original interest centred on the transition from medieval to early modern society in Gwynedd and to this he devoted years of work in the Public Record Office, the National Library and the University College of North Wales, and on legal texts. This led to the realisation that to understand late medieval Wales it was necessary to go back to the period before the conquest and as a result his work shed new light on developments in the thirteenth century. In 'The growth of commutation in thirteenth-century Gwynedd' (1941) he demonstrated the extent to which a money economy had developed by the time of the conquest and his work on the towns of Pwllheli and Nefyn in Llŷn (1941–4, 1957) highlighted the existence of native urban communities in Wales before the coming of Edward I.[36] The result of these studies was a complete reexamination of thirteenth-century Wales, especially of Gwynedd, building on the narrative foundations laid by Lloyd and on the evidence of late medieval extents and accounts; this revealed the changes which were taking place in Gwynedd and how the position of the princes was being built up as part of the attempt to create a principality of Wales and the institutional structure to sustain it. Jones Pierce showed that thirteenth-century Wales was a far more complex society and one far more influenced by developments elsewhere in Europe than had hitherto been assumed. His conclusions were distilled in the lecture 'The age of the princes', published in 1950.[37] Perhaps his outstanding piece of research was 'The *gafael* in Bangor MS

1939' (1942); this closely-argued paper does not make easy reading but it is a masterly example of the way in which a fifteenth-century rental of lands in the Conwy valley could be used alongside contemporary title-deeds and later archival and topographical evidence to reconstruct the medieval tenurial pattern in a single township. He had planned a book on thirteenth-century Wales, but his health was never robust and he died just as it was beginning to take shape in his mind. His contribution was in the shape of articles in various journals; some of the most significant were reprinted in a memorial volume.[38]

Another historian cut off in his prime was Glyn Roberts (1904–62). His early work was on eighteenth-century Welsh electoral politics, but he moved back to the sixteenth century, intending to write a book on Tudor Wales. His academic career was interrupted by war service as a civil servant; after the war he became Professor of Welsh History at Bangor. His experience was similar to that of Jones Pierce; he, too, realised that to understand the sixteenth century, and particularly the leaders of the Welsh community, it was essential to investigate the rise of gentry families through the holding of office and the acquisition of land in the later middle ages. He saw these men as 'supreme pragmatists' and his work revealed the early history of the lineage of Ednyfed Fychan, the ancestors of the Tudor dynasty, and the part which they played in the fourteenth-century principality.[39] He also pursued the history of that branch of the family which stayed at home in Anglesey, making no attempt to take advantage of its kinsman's success in 1485, and declining into extinction.[40] Under his supervision a succession of research students examined the origins of some of the leading families of north Wales, taking advantage of the wealth of family and estate documents at Bangor. But, again like Jones Pierce, he was not spared to produce the book which would have drawn together the threads of his research; a memorial volume assembled his most important articles.[41]

These were the founding fathers of the modern study of the history of medieval Wales, but they were not the only ones.

H. T. Evans's *Wales and the Wars of the Roses* (1915) is a pioneering work which for a long time stood alone. Scholars outside Wales also played their part; the great *Survey of the Honour of Denbigh* of 1334 was edited by Sir Paul Vinogradoff's research seminar at Oxford and published in 1914 under the auspices of the British Academy. In 1926 T. P. Ellis published *Welsh Tribal Law and Custom in the Middle Ages*, a detailed examination of Welsh law studied alongside the evidence of the late medieval extents; Ellis had been a magistrate in the Punjab, an experience which enabled him to see customary law from the inside, but he saw the law of Hywel as something static. It was only after J. G. Edwards's 1928 lecture that the study of Welsh law began its steady advance; since then critical editions of legal texts have been published and regular conferences and seminars have made legal studies one of the most flourishing branches of Welsh scholarship. Historians like Dafydd Jenkins, Thomas Charles-Edwards and Huw Pryce have shed new light on the place of the laws in medieval Wales.[42]

The Contemporary Scene

The study of the history of medieval Wales has not engendered any great debates or produced any school of historians; the plain truth is that it is not a field which has attracted many scholars and much basic work therefore remains to be done. Even in the 1960s students were dependent on the work of Lloyd, with the addition of various articles; the author of a book on the sources of medieval Welsh history, published in 1972, quoted the comment of a lecturer in Welsh history that he had to treat the thirteenth century as a dialogue between himself and Sir John Lloyd.[43] But there was already some movement; in 1962 Glanmor Williams produced *The Welsh Church from Conquest to Reformation*. Glanmor Williams's particular field of study is the sixteenth century but, as he himself admitted, he found himself in the same position as Jones Pierce and Glyn Roberts. His intention had been to write a book on the Reformation in Wales, but to understand it he had to examine the history of the church from 1282 onwards. The result was a work which brought together archival, literary and poetic evidence to paint a rounded picture of the medieval Welsh church and which showed that medieval poetry, described by one reviewer as 'that populous, inaccessible Parnassus which the rest of us must needs see by faith in a dark manner', is an indispensable source for the study of so many aspects of medieval Wales.[44] The upsurge in research in Welsh history generally from the 1970s onwards also owes much to the example and the encouragement of Glanmor Williams.

Since 1970 a new generation of historians has carried on the task. Our understanding of the history of pre-Norman Wales has been revolutionised by the painstaking diplomatic scholarship of Wendy Davies on the Book of Llandaff, a collection of early charter memoranda long dismissed as forgeries.[45] The foundations of the study of the impact of the Normans on Wales were laid by Lloyd and the work has been carried on by David Walker; an American scholar, L. H. Nelson, in *The Normans in South Wales, 1071–1170*, has sought to apply the frontier thesis of the American historian F. J. Turner to the Anglo-Welsh border and J. Le Patourel and W. L. Warren have looked at Wales in the context of the Anglo-Norman polity.[46] In his 1956 discussion of marcher lordship J. G. Edwards suggested that marcher lordship was derived from Welsh kingship and that Norman conquerors stepped into the shoes of the Welsh rulers they displaced; in 1979 R. R. Davies offered a critique of Edwards's arguments, seeing the nature of marcher power and authority as something essentially pragmatic and not at all clear-cut.[47] The one twelfth-century Welsh figure of international standing, Gerald of Wales, has attracted the attention of many scholars, among them David Walker, the German historian Michael Richter, who has discussed Gerald in the context of Welsh national consciousness, and Robert Bartlett, who has looked at him against the contemporary European intellectual background.[48]

It was the seventh centenary of the death of Llywelyn ap Gruffydd in 1982 that gave a great impetus to work on the thirteenth century. The work of Jones Pierce has been carried on by his pupil J. Beverley Smith, one of the most productive of Welsh historians, among whose main interests is Welsh dynastic politics. Professor Smith's main work to date has been his biography of Llywelyn ap Gruffydd, published in Welsh in 1986 (an English version is in preparation).[49] This is in the J. E. Lloyd tradition and offers a completely new interpretation of the thirteenth-century principality, of the nature of Llywelyn's overlordship of his fellow-rulers and his relations with the English crown and of the final crises and the conquest. Professor Smith has examined Welsh political attitudes during the reign of Edward II and the relations of the crown and the community in the northern principality during the reign of Henry VII; he is also one of the small band of scholars who have made an important contribution to the study of the Welsh laws.[50] Among the other historians to have turned their attention to the thirteenth century are David Stephenson who, in *The Governance of Gwynedd* (1984), has examined the whole structure of princely power and government in the principality and the men who were the executants of the prince's policy, and the late Keith Williams-Jones, whose edition of *The Merioneth Lay Subsidy Roll, 1292–93* (1976) includes an introduction which is in itself a study of the social and economic background of Llywelyn ap Gruffydd's principality.[51] Dr Llinos Beverley Smith has examined the narrative account of Llywelyn ap Gruffydd's death and subsequent perceptions of the last prince and has also published the detailed list of grievances of the community of north Wales against Llywelyn laid before royal officials in 1283.[52] Scholars who are better-known for their contributions in other areas have also written on the thirteenth-century princes; Ceri Lewis examined the 1247 Treaty of Woodstock in detail, putting it in its historical context, and in 1964 Gwyn A. Williams published a characteristically perceptive study of the political consequences of the death of Llywelyn ab Iorwerth in 1240 and the succession to Gwynedd.[53]

In his contribution to the *festschrift* presented to Glanmor Williams in 1984, R. R. Davies examined the question of national identity in thirteenth-century Wales.[54] He suggested that Welsh law, the law of Hywel Dda, was an integral part of this development and was used by the princes, particularly Llywelyn ap Gruffydd, to this end. Professor Davies has also studied the survival of Welsh law and procedure in the later middle ages and he has been one of the pioneers of a new development in British historical studies, the study of the history of the British Isles and their four component nations as a whole.[55] As far as medieval history is concerned the first public manifestation of this approach may have ben a conference of Welsh, Scottish and Irish historians in 1986, the proceedings of which were subsequently published under Professor Davies's editorship.[56] This was followed in 1990 by two books, *Domination and Conquest: the experience of Ireland, Scotland and Wales, 1100-1300*, by Professor Davies himself, and *The Political Development of the British Isles, 1100–1400*, by Robin Frame, a specialist in medieval Irish history. These leaps over the walls which have tended to divide the historians of England and the three Celtic countries have carried forward the earlier work of Le Patourel and Warren and moved away from the self-contained approach of so many scholars in the past. Typical of this 'new British history' is the paper given at the 1986 conference by the Irish historian J. F. Lydon, 'Lordship and crown: Llywelyn of Wales and O'Connor of Connacht', which compares the relations of the English crown in the thirteenth century with the house of Gwynedd and the kings of Connacht.[57]

The period after 1282 has attracted fewer historians in recent years. R. R. Davies's *Lordship and Society in the March of Wales, 1282–1400* (1978) is a detailed study of government, law and society in the march, based on a wide range of archival sources. The administrative history of the principality has yet to be written in its entirety, although as long ago as 1935 W. H. Waters published *The Edwardian Settlement of North Wales in its administrative and legal aspects, 1284–1343*. However, Ralph Griffiths has produced the first volume of a prosopography of office-holders with a detailed introduction; this volume deals with the southern principality and its northern counterpart is in preparation.[58] Some local studies have appeared but most recent work is in the form of articles. There are also several theses on particular marcher lordships which will, one hopes, emerge eventually as monographs; the same point can be made about other topics. The Glyn Dŵr revolt is a seam which is far from exhausted; Lloyd's book is still the starting point but R. R. Davies's 1968 article 'Owain Glyn Dŵr and the Welsh squirearchy' shed new light on the web of family connections which lay behind the involvement of so many of the *uchelwyr*.[59] Several local studies of the revolt have added to our knowledge, among them J. E. Messham's study of it in Flintshire, based on the immensely rich Palatinate of Chester records in the Public Record Office and R. K. Turvey's investigation of its course in Pembrokeshire; Keith Williams-Jones's detailed account of the capture of Conwy castle in 1401 was a foretaste of that examination of law and order in fifteenth-century Wales which will sadly never now appear.[60] A short book by Glanmor Williams on Owain Glyn Dŵr made its first appearance in 1966, but there is a need for a large-scale work on the revolt as a whole.

The fifteenth century is a period which Ralph Griffiths has made his own in the shape of a number of important articles, mainly on the political dimension and on questions of lordship, patronage and government.[61] He has also edited a collection of studies of medieval Welsh boroughs; Ian Soulsby's *The Towns of Medieval Wales* (1983) has provided a useful gazeteer of medieval urban settlements, but there is a great deal of virgin soil waiting to be tilled in this area.[62] In the sphere of agrarian history the medieval volumes of the *Agrarian History of England and Wales* have dealt with Wales in some detail and have provided a starting point for further work.[63] Important contributions have been made by scholars in other disciplines, particularly the historical geographer Glanville Jones, whose use of medieval surveys and extents has cast light on earlier periods, and by a number of specialists on medieval Welsh literature, including D. J. Bowen, G. Aled Williams, Eurys Rowlands and Dafydd Johnston. The amount of work done in recent years, coupled with the new approach to the history of the British Isles, has led to new works of synthesis. The Oxford History of Wales, a joint

venture by the Oxford University Press and the University of
Wales Press, includes two substantial volumes, R. R. Davies's
Conquest, Coexistence and Change: Wales, 1063–1415 (1987) and
Glanmor Williams's *Recovery, Reorientation and Reformation: Wales,
c. 1415–1642*, published in the same year.

This discussion of work on medieval Wales reads like a
catalogue and no apology is offered for that; there are so few
working in this field and so much basic work is still to be done
that signposts are necessary to indicate how much opportunity
remains for individual historians to make significant and original
contributions. With so much fresh ground still to be broken there
has been little scope for the kind of debates which have
developed in other fields. The only real historiographical debate
has been over the causes of the breakdown in Anglo-Welsh
political relations in the late thirteenth century and the conquest
of 1282–3. Perceptions of Llywelyn ap Gruffydd have changed
over the centuries; a series of articles in the Welsh journal *Y
Faner* in the autumn of 1982 by the literary historian Hywel Teifi
Edwards examined Welsh views of him in the nineteenth
century. Earlier writers had seen him as an outstanding patriotic
leader; this was, in a way, true of J. E. Lloyd, for whom the
Treaty of Montgomery in 1267 was the high point of his
achievement. Lloyd did not give much space to the subsequent
crises and wars or to the conquest itself; his Llywelyn has many
of the characteristics of a tragic hero overwhelmed by fate. The
first real study of the period after Montgomery was that by J. G.
Edwards in his introduction to *Littere Wallie* (1940) in which he
examined what Llywelyn was trying to do. Edwards argued that
the prince must bear the ultimate blame for the deterioration in
relations after the accession of Edward I in 1272; he misjudged
his man and he misjudged the situation in England, believing
that the kingdom was still weak after the civil war of the previous
decade. He took no account of the internal stresses and strains of
his own principality and he ignored the terms of a treaty which
he had sought in the first place. He was, in short, foolhardy and
irresponsible. After 1277 he was faced with an impossible
situation; once Dafydd had begun the war in 1282 he had no

choice but to join to control it and to protect his own position as prince.[64]

If Edwards laid the blame squarely at Llywelyn's door, J. Conway Davies, in the introduction to *The Welsh Assize Roll*, published in the same year, argued that Edward must bear all the responsibility for what happened in 1282. He maintained that the king was determined to destroy Llywelyn and conquer his principality; he interpreted everything to his own advantage and pushed the prince too hard. Llywelyn had no choice but to resist and the conquest was the result; this was exactly what Edward was looking for.[65] A more subtle interpretation was put forward by Sir Maurice Powicke in 1947 in *King Henry III and the Lord Edward*.[66] To him the cause of the crisis lay in a conflict of laws, a clash between two concepts of legal right. Edward's aim was to define and clarify Anglo-Welsh relations once and for all; the problem was that he and Llywelyn had different conceptions of the nature of royal overlordship. The Aberconwy settlement was harsh but fair; the roots of further trouble lay in the north-east where misgovernment by royal officials was compounded by a misunderstanding of the nuances of Welsh law and custom. As a result Dafydd ap Gruffydd was able to take advantage of the unease of Welsh lords outside the principality in 1282 and this led to the final disaster.

Subsequent interpretations of the conquest have moved away from the apportionment of blame and have examined the motives of the protagonists in far greater detail. In a lecture delivered in 1969 the late S. B. Chrimes argued that the key factor was Llywelyn's refusal to perform the homage which he had undertaken to do in an agreed treaty.[67] For R. R. Davies the problem was the irreconcilable clash of Edward's 'imperious, even imperial' view of his overlordship and Llywelyn's vision of a Welsh principality, coupled with the extension of English suzerainty over the British Isles.[68] J. Beverley Smith sees the size of Llywelyn's principality as one of his problems; it was a mistake for him to have moved into the march in the early 1260s and he would have been wiser to have settled for Gwynedd, Powys and Deheubarth, although it should be added that he had little choice at the time.[69] Professor Smith has provided the most detailed and the most sensitive account of the succession of crises which led ultimately to the fall of Llywelyn ap Gruffydd, but it is unlikely that the last word has been written about 1282; the debate goes on.[70]

2

THE NORMAN CHALLENGE

The Political Background

By the eleventh century there were four main kingdoms in Wales, Gwynedd in the north, Powys in the centre, Deheubarth in the south-west and Morgannwg or Glamorgan in the south-east. The first two had a history going back to the departure of the Romans, if not earlier; Morgannwg was created in the eighth century and Deheubarth in the tenth by one of the most famous Welsh kings, Hywel Dda. There had in the past been various lesser kingdoms on the periphery of the large ones but most of these were gradually absorbed by their powerful neighbours. Political boundaries were, to a large extent, dictated by physical geography; internal natural frontiers always played a significant part in the history of Wales and they are still obvious today. Internal communications have never been easy and there was no central region which could serve as a focus for unity. Loyalties were to local rulers and there was no compelling reason to look beyond the borders of the individual kingdom. Gwynedd, with its central defensive core of Snowdonia, was always potentially the most powerful element in Welsh politics but, like the other kingdoms, it was often riven by dynastic in-fighting. Before 1064 only four rulers had been able to extend their power over a substantial part of Wales; these were Rhodri Mawr (d. 878) and Gruffydd ap Llywelyn (d. 1064) of Gwynedd and Hywel Dda (d. 950) and Maredudd ab Owain (d. 999) of Deheubarth.[1]

Unlike England and Scotland, Wales did not experience that process of political coalescence which led to the emergence of a single kingdom and kingship. In Scotland Kenneth mac Alpin had begun to do this by the middle of the ninth century and in England the final conquest of the Scandinavian kingdom of York in 954 made Eadred of Wessex the first real king of the English. The precocious unity of England was really the result of the Danish invasions in the ninth century; these destroyed the kingships of East Anglia, Mercia and Northumbria, leaving only Wessex in a position to fight back and eventually to unite England under its rule. Like the rest of western Europe, Wales felt the impact of Viking attacks but there was no attempt at conquest or settlement as there was in England; its economic resources were probably not worth the effort. It is, however, possible that Gwynedd was subject to some kind of Scandinavian overlordship in the late tenth and early eleventh centuries; given the fact that the Irish Sea was, to all intents and purposes, a Viking lake, this would hardly have been surprising.[2]

Political struggles could be violent and sanguinary; between 949 and 1066 the main Welsh chronicle records the violent ends of no fewer than 35 rulers, more often at the hands of their compatriots than at those of the English or Vikings.[3] This does not reflect any inherent instability in the Welsh political culture; it was usually a consequence of dynastic rivalry in a world in which any member of the royal kindred might consider himself a legitimate contender for political power. Gruffydd ap Llywelyn is reputed to have justified the elimination of his rivals with the words 'I kill no one; I merely blunt the horns of the children of Wales lest they injure their mother'.[4] And such dynastic violence was certainly not exclusive to Wales.

Welsh politics could not but be affected by the English presence to the east. Offa of Mercia may be said to have defined the two nations by the construction of the earthwork which bears his name at the end of the eighth century and some southern rulers had sought the protection of Alfred the Great against Anarawd ap Rhodri of Gwynedd a hundred years later.[5] Athelstan of Wessex is said to have imposed his overlordship on the Welsh at a meeting at Hereford in 927. Athelstan saw himself as a kind of emperor or over-king of Britain and Hywel Dda and other Welsh rulers were summoned from time to time to his court where they witnessed some of his grandiloquent charters and may have learned something from his example of visible and splendid kingship. Welsh rulers do seem usually to have been quite prepared to accept some kind of external suzerainty; this may have a long history, even going back to the concept of the Roman province of Britain, and it lies at the heart of the Arthurian tradition. This did not mean that relations were invariably friendly; a prophetic poem called *Armes Prydein*, possibly composed about 930, calls for a grand alliance of the Welsh, the Cornish, the Scots and the Norsemen to drive out the Saxons and recover Britain for the Britons.[6]

It was suzerainty rather than conquest that concerned Anglo-Saxon rulers in their dealings with Wales; the story of Edgar being rowed on the Dee at Chester by Welsh and Scottish tributary kings may reflect such a relationship. Until 954 the West Saxon kings' priority was the reconquest of those parts of England that had been lost to the Danes and towards the end of the century the Scandinavian threat returned. Only when Welsh rulers tried to become involved in English politics were they perceived as a threat. At the end of the ninth century Anarawd of Gwynedd had had a short-lived alliance with the Vikings of York; had this alliance endured it could have menaced West Saxon ambitions by creating a band of hostile territory extending from the North Sea to the Irish Sea and beyond. Gruffydd ap Llywelyn's later alliance with Earl Aelfgar of Mercia created a powerful bloc between the power-bases of Harold Godwinson in Wessex and his brother Tostig in Northumbria at a time when Harold was beginning to see himself as successor to the childless Edward the Confessor; this was enough to make the destruction of Gruffydd in 1064 imperative.

Political authority in a Welsh kingdom lay with the king; he might seek the advice of those who knew the law and the precedents but his was the final word. The court, composed of the king and a body of officials with a large retinue, travelled regularly around the kingdom, being maintained by the fruits of the labour of the bondmen on the local demesne and the food renders, labour services and billeting obligations of the rest of the king's subjects. The king was chosen from among the members of the royal kindred during the lifetime of his predecessor; the kindred was a four-generation group, which meant that eligibility involved being at least the great-grandson of a king. He was the enforcer of law and justice and the custodian of public order; he was also the source of patronage and was expected to be open-handed and generous, especially to the church and to poets. There was no administrative structure comparable to the elaborate pattern of shire and hundred which had developed in Anglo-Saxon England by 1000, although each kingdom was made up of a number of cantrefs, most of which were later subdivided into commotes.

The Coming of the Normans

The death of Harold Godwinson at Hastings and the Norman conquest of England was bound to affect Wales. Even before the death of Edward the Confessor Normans had appeared on the Welsh border; as early as 1051 the king's Norman nephew Ralph of Mantes had become earl of Hereford and others had followed him. It was some years before the conquerors reached the border but by 1071 William the Conqueror had created three new earldoms, based on Hereford, Shrewsbury and Chester, and had bestowed them on trusted servants experienced in the defence of border areas in Normandy. These three centres controlled the main routes into Wales, but it is unlikely that the original purpose of the three earldoms was to serve as springboards for further invasion and conquest. There were to be territorial conquests but what William sought was a secure frontier; he was aware that Welsh rulers, among them Gruffydd ap Llywelyn, had had close relations with the Hiberno-Norse kingdom of Dublin and he was also aware that his victory at Hastings had been preceded by the defeat and death of Harald Hardrada of

Norway at Stamford Bridge. The Scandinavian threat remained and William understood this very well.

The conquest of Wales and Scotland was no part of William's plan. When he crossed the English Channel in the autumn of 1066 he came to claim his lawful inheritance as the heir of his great-uncle Edward the Confessor who, he alleged, had promised him the succession. He therefore saw himself as the legitimate successor of the West Saxon kings, inheriting the position of Athelstan and Edgar as well as that of Edward; this meant that he inherited their relationship with the Welsh, which did not involve the expansion of English territory. His relations with Malcolm III of Scotland were clarified in the Treaty of Abernethy of 1072, under which Malcolm gave him hostages and did homage; in Wales there was no single ruler with whom he could come to such an agreement, but his main preoccupation was stability and a secure border and it may have been Welsh support for rebels in England between 1067 and 1069 that had led him to establish the border earldoms.

It was not long before Normans appeared on Welsh soil. The first Welsh reference to them comes from *Brut y Tywysogyon* in the year 1072, when the chronicle records the death in battle of Maredudd ab Owain of Deheubarth at the hands of Caradog ap Gruffydd of Gwent and the 'French'.[7] What we have here is the involvement of Normans in Welsh politics, not as conquerors but as the allies of one of the participants in a struggle between two kingdoms; in other words they were just one more element in a complicated Welsh political patchwork which at different times in the eleventh century had involved West Saxons, Mercians and Hiberno-Norsemen, in addition to the various native kingdoms. Another example of this was the consecration, some time after 1075, of the new chapel in the castle of Monmouth by a Welsh bishop in the presence of King Caradog; this episode reflects early Norman settlement from Hereford into the adjacent Welsh kingdom of Gwent.[8] Some Normans had established forward bases beyond the three border towns from the beginning. William fitz Osbern, the new earl of Hereford, built a castle at Strigoil or Chepstow, while Roger of Montgomery, earl of

Shrewsbury, erected the castle which bore his name on the Severn, and Robert of Rhuddlan, a kinsman of the earl of Chester, established himself at Rhuddlan. These forward bases did not, however, involve movement into Wales; at this time they were all on the English side of the border.

Although conquest was not on the king's agenda, this did not deter individual Normans from making bids for political power in Wales. The evidence in Domesday Book helps to explain how the process of penetration operated. What the king sought in Wales was stability. The way to secure this was by making agreements or treaties with recognised Welsh rulers, as he had done with Malcolm III. The outstanding example of this process comes from Domesday Book; here it is recorded that south Wales was held of the king by a certain 'Riset' who paid an annual tribute of £40.[9] 'Riset' was probably Rhys ap Tewdwr of Deheubarth. In 1081 William led an army through south Wales as far as St David's; according to Welsh sources his intention on this, his only visit to Wales, was to pay his respects to the saint but it is far more likely to have been a demonstration in strength, possibly in response to the victory of Rhys and Gruffydd ap Cynan of Gwynedd at Mynydd Carn in the same year. In this battle they had, with the aid of a force of mercenaries from Dublin, defeated and killed the intrusive rulers of Deheubarth and Gwynedd and recovered their patrimonies; it may have been the presence of Scandinavian mercenaries on British soil that had alarmed William and caused him to lead an army into Wales. The result of this campaign may have been a meeting with Rhys where he did homage and agreed to pay the tribute. For the king such an agreement could secure stability in south-west Wales; for Rhys it meant security. Recognised as he now was by William and with a formal relationship with him, no Norman adventurer would dare threaten Deheubarth or its ruler.

This argument may be supported by the Domesday evidence from Gwynedd. Here Robert of Rhuddlan was described as holding north Wales at farm, also for an annual payment of £40; he held other lands there as well.[10] If the £40 paid by 'Riset' was a traditional tribute payable to the English crown by the ruler of Deheubarth, the payment due from Robert of Rhuddlan may have been a similar one from Gwynedd. This suggests that by 1086 Robert was recognised by the king as ruler of Gwynedd by right of conquest. How had this come about? In 1063 Bleddyn ap Cynfyn had sworn fealty, as ruler of Gwynedd, to Edward the Confessor; this meant that he was recognised and William had inherited Edward's relationship with him. Consequently no Norman intruder could challenge his position. But Bleddyn was killed by Rhys ab Owain of Deheubarth in 1075 and his place in Gwynedd was taken by another intruder, his cousin Trahaearn ap Caradog of the small mid-Wales kingdom of Arwystli. This was the signal for the heir of the legitimate Gwynedd dynasty, Gruffydd ap Cynan ab Iago, an exile brought up near Dublin, to make a bid for his inheritance. He invaded Gwynedd and seized power from Trahaearn with the assistance of a body of mercenaries and Robert of Rhuddlan. But his mercenaries showed a serious lack of discipline and many of them were slaughtered in their camp by the men of Llŷn.[11] Gruffydd was forced to return to Ireland and Trahaearn recovered Gwynedd. In 1081 Gruffydd and his fellow-exile Rhys ap Tewdwr, the claimant to Deheubarth, came back to Wales, again with a force of mercenaries from Dublin and at Mynydd Carn, somewhere in south-west Wales, they defeated and killed Trahaearn and Caradog ap Gruffydd, who had seized power in Deheubarth.[12] Rhys was restored to power but Gruffydd, on his way back to Gwynedd, was captured by the Normans and imprisoned in Chester. The result was a power vacuum in Gwynedd and it was at this point that Robert of Rhuddlan probably moved in. There was no legitimate native ruler there; there had been no ruler recognised by the king of England since 1075. Power was there for the taking by whoever had the enterprise to seize it. There was no reason why an adventurer like Robert of Rhuddlan should not make a bid for the kingship; if a Norman had seized the kingship of England in 1066, another could do the same thing in Gwynedd twenty years later. No Norman would venture to challenge the position of a Welsh ruler recognised by and having treaty relations with King William, but when there was a vacancy or a disputed succession any competitor might make a bid for power and, if successful, be recognised by the king and pay the necessary tribute.

This period of relative stability in Anglo-Welsh relations came to an end with William's death in 1087. His successor William II was not bound by his father's agreements and he needed the support of the Norman lords on the border in the face of his elder brother Robert of Normandy's bid for the crown. The change can be seen very clearly in the fate of Deheubarth. One of the Normans now established in Herefordshire was Bernard de Neufmarché, the son-in-law of one of the pre-1066 Norman settlers, Osbern fitz Richard, who had married a daughter of Gruffydd ap Llywelyn. Bernard had begun to move along the Wye into the small Welsh kingdom of Brycheiniog and his advance set alarm bells ringing in Deheubarth. Brycheiniog was probably seen as a kind of buffer zone between Deheubarth and the English border and any change in its position would therefore have been perceived as a threat further west. By 1093 Bernard had reached Aberhonddu, the later Brecon. Rhys ap Tewdwr must have felt obliged to respond and in that year he was killed at Aberhonddu. The significance of his death was understood; *Brut y Tywysogyon* said of it 'and then fell the kingdom of the Britons'.[13] Rhys's death meant the end of a clearly-defined and workable political relationship between the king of England and individual Welsh rulers, at least for the time being.

With the death of Rhys ap Tewdwr the floodgates were opened. Before long the whole of Brycheiniog was in the possession of Bernard de Neufmarché and Deheubarth was the next to fall. But it did not, as one might have expected, fall to a Norman advance from Hereford and Brecon. From Shrewsbury a son of Earl Roger, Arnulf of Montgomery, moved westwards along the Severn and through the Talerddig gap to reach the shores of Cardigan Bay; from here the Normans swept down through Ceredigion, building a castle and founding a borough at Pembroke. The constable of the new castle, Gerald of Windsor, and his descendants were to leave their imprint on both Wales and Ireland. Pembroke was to be the symbol of Norman power in south-west Wales and it never once fell to the Welsh. There was also movement into mid-Wales; by 1095 Philip de Braose was established at Radnor and before long he had occupied the cantref of Buellt. But the greatest Norman gain was Glamorgan. This began during the last decade of the eleventh century and was the work of Robert fitz Hamo, whose power-base was in Bristol and Gloucestershire. The circumstances of this conquest are not altogether clear but the initial invasion may have been connected with a disputed succession. It involved the conquest of the Vale of Glamorgan; fitz Hamo's new castle at Cardiff became the seat of lordship and those native Welsh rulers of the uplands who had previously been subject to the Welsh king now became his vassals, along with some of the knights who had come with him. He died in 1107, having lost his reason after being wounded in battle; his daughter and sole heiress was married by Henry I to his illegitimate son Robert of Gloucester. The lordship remained in the possession of the earls of Gloucester until the fourteenth century. The extension of the lord's authority over the upland lords was a long process, not completed until the second half of the thirteenth century, when it was to have considerable repercussions and to contribute to that series of crises in Anglo-Welsh relations which led ultimately to the conquest of 1282.

The Norman advance was not limited to south Wales. In Gwynedd the capture and imprisonment of Gruffydd ap Cynan in 1081 had led to the position recorded in Domesday Book. After Robert of Rhuddlan's death his place was taken by the earl of Chester, and in the early 1090s the Norman hold was so strong that a Breton, Hervé, became bishop in Gwynedd, lands in Anglesey were granted to the monks of Chester, and castles were built there and at Bangor and Caernarfon. Domesday Book also shows much of eastern Powys either in Norman hands or under Norman overlordship, exercised from Shrewsbury. The process continued in the early years of Henry I's reign with new Norman lordships like Gower and Gydweli being established in the south-west and the first royal castle in Wales being founded at Carmarthen in 1109. In 1108 many Flemings, driven from their homeland by a natural disaster, were settled by the king in the southern part of Dyfed.[14] These were colonists, not conquerors, and they soon left their stamp on the region; the linguistic boundary or *landsker* which followed this settlement is clearly defined to this day. By the end of Henry's reign in 1135 practically the whole of south Wales was under Norman rule; this was the greatest threat that the Welsh had yet had to face.

The Making of the March

The result of the Norman advance was the creation of the march. The word itself means a border area or frontier region but in Wales it came to have a particular meaning as a result of the establishment of marcher lordships. The term is, in some ways, an emotive one; the marcher lordships of the later middle ages were long seen as a world of over-mighty subjects and privileged lords exercising royal authority in their own interest. In fact they were Welsh lordships in Wales, ruled by Anglo-Norman lords by right of conquest and lying between England and those parts of Wales under native Welsh rule (*Pura Wallia*). In no way were they part of the kingdom of England, nor were they a kind of no man's land between England and Wales; they owed their origin to nothing more than the Norman advance into Wales.

The origins of the powers exercised by marcher lords have been explained in different ways over the centuries. According to the sixteenth-century Pembrokeshire antiquary George Owen of Henllys, William the Conqueror had given the lords he established on the Anglo-Welsh border a free hand to serve as a barrier against Welsh attacks.[15] Any territory they conquered they could keep because they were England's first line of defence. But this argument has long been seen as inadequate and a more sophisticated one was put forward by Sir Goronwy Edwards in 1956.[16] He compared the powers and authority of the Anglo-Norman marcher lord with those of the native Welsh king and saw them as identical. When a Welsh kingdom or lordship was conquered, the conqueror stepped into the shoes of the ruler he had displaced. The basic unit of political and territorial authority was the commote and Sir Goronwy saw this as the unit of conquest. Marcher lordship was therefore no more and no less than Welsh kingship in Anglo-Norman hands. The debate has been further refined by R. R. Davies who has argued that the march was a pragmatic world where authority was not based on constitutional theory; attempts to explain it came later.[17] For ambitious Normans on the border Wales was a land of opportunity not under the authority of the English crown. If a Welsh ruler had no formal relationship with the king of England or if a succession was in dispute, there were no constraints. A Norman adventurer could do in Wales what he could not do in England; he could make war for personal gain in what was essentially a land of war. The Norman advance into Wales was a military matter, not a constitutional one. In the march these lords exercised Welsh political authority because that was what they found there; they took what they needed from the existing local pattern and greed and ambition took precedence over political theory and law. One distinctive feature of marcher lordship was the right of the lords to levy private war against their neighbours; this was inherited from their Welsh predecessors and was a symbol of their independence. And for them this was also a feudal world; in a frontier zone military service and sheer military power were of paramount importance. The Normans had a particular talent for adopting the customs and habits of the people among whom they settled; they were the chameleons of medieval Europe.

The first step in the process of conquest was the building of a castle. This was a sign of independence; in England the king kept a firm hand on private castle-building. It was also a symbol of military insecurity which showed that the march was a war-zone where the threat of hostilities was always present and it was the visible and concrete emblem of conquest, serving as the base for its consolidation. The Norman method of warfare, developed in Normandy, was based on castles and open country. The earliest castles were simple motte-and-bailey structures, consisting of an earthen mound surmounted by a wooden tower and surrounded by an enclosure with an earthen rampart; Hen Domen near Montgomery is one of the best examples but many mottes are still to be seen, especially in mid-Wales.[18] Many were no more than temporary structures, marking the path of conquest, but some would later be rebuilt in stone. Once a lordship was established, the lord's castle became a combination of military headquarters and seat of government. Around it a small town grew up to serve as a trading centre to supply its needs and to help, when necessary, in its defence. This was the origin of most historic Welsh towns; examples include Cardiff, Swansea, Brecon and Haverfordwest. The earliest inhabitants of these towns were English settlers, often brought from the lord's lands in England; Cardiff, for example, had particular links with Tewkesbury, also on the lands of Robert fitz Hamo.[19] As towns developed, they would receive charters of incorporation from their lords and many of them came to have a substantial Welsh element in their population.

In lordships like Glamorgan where there was extensive fertile land there might also be a degree of English rural settlement and here a manorial structure might develop. This part of the lordship would be known as the Englishry, but it only existed where the land was suitable for such a form of agrarian organisation. Welsh tenants were not usually evicted but lived under the custom of the manor; English settlers were often absorbed within a few generations. The rest of the lordship was known as the Welshry; here Welsh tenures continued, traditional renders and services remained, but paid to the marcher lord rather than to the Welsh ruler, and Welsh law was administered in Welsh courts by Welsh officials. The lord's central administration in the castle often had both English officials to deal with English tenants and Welsh officials to deal with Welsh ones. But it is important to remember that, as every marcher lordship was independent, so was every marcher lordship different; there was a world of difference between the largest, Glamorgan, which contained many sub-lordships, some of which might have their own Englishries and Welshries, and an upland lordship like

Elfael in mid-Wales. In the early days of marcher lordship the lord might often be resident but later, as more and more lordships passed by marriage or inheritance into the possession of English magnates, lords tended to be absentees, treating their Welsh lordships as a source of income and leaving administration in the hands of local officials, many of whom were Welsh.

For many Welshmen, then, the coming of the Normans meant a change of ruler, although they did not come under the authority of the English crown; their new lords owed homage to the king but they were, at the same time, independent rulers and very jealous of their independence. It was a maxim of English law that the king's writ did not run in the march. In practical terms there was little change for most of the new lord's tenants but in parts of lowland Wales the new order did have some impact on the landscape. In a period when the climate was particularly favourable more land was brought into cultivation. Castles, too, contributed to the landscape and nucleated villages reflected large-scale arable farming, although it was not the Normans who, as has sometimes been suggested, introduced such farming to Wales. Earlier sources indicate the growing of crops and the existence of some substantial estates, particularly in the south-east; the manorial organisation introduced by the Normans may well have been little different from what had gone before. Cattle, however, continued to be the mainstay of the upland economy and *cymorth*, originally a render of cattle, was one of the main payments due to a marcher lord from upland communities.[20] The landscape in the Englishry could be one of nucleated villages around their churches, while that in the Welshry was generally one of scattered farms, although the nucleated community could have been rather more common in Wales before the havoc wrought by plague and depopulation in the fourteenth and fifteenth centuries.

The Welsh Response

The Norman advance did not go unchallenged. Although Gruffydd ap Cynan had been captured and imprisoned by the

Normans after his victory at Mynydd Carn in 1081, he appears to have been free by 1090 and it was possibly in 1093 that he killed Robert of Rhuddlan in a surprise attack on Robert's castle at Degannwy on the Conwy estuary.[21] The first large-scale Welsh response came in 1094 when a major war broke out in both north and south Wales when the king, William Rufus, was absent in France. It petered out in the south after the failure of the Welsh to capture the key fortress of Pembroke, saved by a ruse on the part of its constable Gerald of Windsor; in the north, led by Gruffydd ap Cynan, now restored to power in Gwynedd, and Cadwgan ap Bleddyn ap Cynfyn of Powys, it was far more successful despite two abortive campaigns, led by the king himself, in 1095 and 1097. But in 1098 Gwynedd was invaded by Earl Hugh of Chester and his namesake, the new earl of Shrewsbury. The fleet from Dublin which Gruffydd and Cadwgan had hired for their defence was bribed by the Normans to change sides; the two princes fled to Ireland and Anglesey was ravaged by the earls. Providence now appeared to take a hand. Magnus Bareleg, the king of Norway, was cruising in the Irish Sea and arrived on the scene. The result was a battle in which the earl of Shrewsbury was killed; the consequence of the battle of Anglesey Sound (probably Beaumaris Bay) was the withdrawal of the Normans, who probably realised that their lines of communication were dangerously exposed and that the Scandinavian threat was still a very real one. It is hard to see Magnus's sudden appearance as a coincidence, especially in the light of Gruffydd's Hiberno-Norse connections; the *deus ex machina* is not really a credible historical figure.

Within the year Gruffydd and Cadwgan had returned and peace had been restored. The centre of gravity of Welsh politics now moved for a time to Powys; most of Deheubarth was in Norman hands and Gruffydd ap Cynan maintained a low profile as he consolidated his position in Gwynedd. The position of Powys was temporarily strengthened by the collapse of the earldom of Shrewsbury. Robert of Bellême, the brother and successor of Hugh, rebelled against Henry I and sought the aid of Cadwgan ap Bleddyn and his brothers. They were suborned by the king and Robert and his brother Arnulf were defeated and exiled. To take Arnulf's place in Dyfed the king chose Gerald of Windsor, who married Henry's former mistress Nest, the daughter of Rhys ap Tewdwr; this was a political marriage, the purpose of which was to give Gerald a strong social and political position in south-west Wales. The power-vacuum left on the border by the fall of Earl Robert was filled for a time by Powys. But this kingdom was bedevilled by dynastic rivalries and Cadwgan ap Bleddyn did not have the strength to impose his authority on his kinsmen. In 1109 his son and heir Owain abducted Nest and the result was an explosion; Henry was forced to intervene and father and son were exiled. For the next few years the king sought stability in vain; eventually Cadwgan had to be reinstated but in 1111 he was killed by his nephew Madog ap Rhirid who had, earlier in the same year, already accounted for Cadwgan's brother Iorwerth. This dynastic blood-bath continued for several years, but it was Owain ap Cadwgan who ultimately emerged as ruler of Powys. Owain does seem to have restored order and in 1115 he went with the king to Normandy and was knighted, being probably the first Welsh-man ever to receive the accolade.[22] In 1116 Owain was one of several Welsh rulers campaigning in south Wales against Gruffydd ap Rhys, the son of Rhŷs ap Tewdwr. Near Carmarthen he was overtaken by a body of Flemings from Pembroke who had several scores to settle with him, along with Gerald of Windsor; Owain was killed and Gerald's cuckolding was avenged.[23] Control of Powys eventually passed to Bleddyn ap Cynfyn's last surviving son Maredudd and he ruled undisturbed until his death in 1132.

Despite his problems with the Powys dynasty, Henry I was one of the most effective and masterful English kings in his dealings with Wales and the Welsh; the author of *Brut y Tywysogyon* described him as 'the man against whom none can contend save God himself'.[24] In 1114 he invaded Gwynedd; Gruffydd ap Cynan and Owain ap Cadwgan were obliged to come to terms, but the campaign was essentially a warning, as was a further invasion in 1121, this time aimed at Maredudd ap

Bleddyn of Powys. In 1115 Gruffydd ap Rhys led a revolt in Deheubarth; this was suppressed but Gruffydd survived in a small part of his ancestral lands to keep the flame alive. But Gwynedd was now in a position to expand. Gruffydd ap Cynan was well-established and his sons were grown to manhood and by 1120 his kingdom was extending its borders and moving into those peripheral areas like Meirionnydd and Rhos which had earlier been subject to Powys. It was reaching new natural frontiers, the Dyfi to the south and the Clwyd to the east.

The situation changed dramatically on the death of Henry I in 1135; within a month war had broken out in south Wales and much territory was rapidly regained by the Welsh. This recovery was facilitated by the disputed succession in England; Henry's nephew Stephen of Blois had been elected king but his daughter, the Empress Matilda, had a strong body of support, much of it in the march. The resulting civil war meant that Welsh rulers had a free hand in recovering their lands. Most of Deheubarth was won back early in 1136. Gruffydd ap Cynan died in 1137, as did Gruffydd ap Rhys of Deheubarth, his son-in-law and the son of his old comrade-in-arms. The former was probably over eighty. He had started from nothing as an exile in Ireland; in Gwynedd he had borne the brunt of the Norman threat and had survived. The biography composed after his death describes his chequered career and paints a picture of peace and prosperity during his later years.[25] He was succeeded by his son Owain, known as Owain Gwynedd, one of the greatest members of a dynasty whose history is the history of independent Wales; with Madog ap Maredudd in Powys and Rhys ap Gruffydd in Deheubarth as well as Owain Gwynedd, Wales was particularly fortunate in its rulers in the twelfth century.

Wales and Henry II

On the death of Stephen in 1154 Matilda's son Henry II became king of England. Henry was one of the greatest of all English kings and it was in his reign that a new stability was achieved in

Anglo-Welsh relations. This stability did not come overnight; in the early part of Henry's reign Wales was invaded several times. Henry II ruled far more than England; as duke of Normandy and Aquitaine and count of Anjou his dominions extended from the Pyrenees to the Cheviots and this conditioned his attitude towards Wales. His main concern on all his borders was stability and this led him to intervene on more than one occasion, the first time being in 1157. This campaign was the result of a further advance to the east by Gwynedd into the lands between the Clwyd and the Dee. This was a region that had been part of England since the ninth century and which, as Domesday Book shows, had a strong English element in its population. But now there was a Welsh reconquest; English place-names took on Welsh forms which they have never lost. Moston, for example, became Mostyn, Soughton near Mold became Sychdyn and Hull became Rhyl. Owain Gwynedd's advance, however, brought the eastern frontier of Gwynedd dangerously close to Chester, the young earl of which was the king's ward. A Welsh presence so close to a city so strategically sensitive was unacceptable and Henry responded. His expedition was not an unqualified success; the army which advanced from Chester came very near to disaster in a Welsh ambush, while the fleet sent to attack Anglesey suffered a crushing defeat in the battle of Tal Moelfre on the Menai Straits. Nevertheless Owain Gwynedd withdrew to the Clwyd, gave hostages and did homage; this was the first occasion on which a Welsh ruler actually did homage to the king of England. South Wales was also invaded, twice in 1158, in 1159 and in 1163; three of these expeditions were led by the king himself. They were all precipitated by the activities of Rhys ap Gruffydd ap Rhys, now ruler of Deheubarth; on each occasion Rhys submitted but each time he resumed his attacks on his marcher neighbours as soon as the royal army had withdrawn. In 1163 he was imprisoned but the ensuing instability in south Wales soon led to his reinstatement after doing homage to Henry at Woodstock along with Owain Gwynedd and Malcolm IV of Scotland. The following year he was active again and this time he was joined by Owain. Henry's response was to prepare a campaign to deal with these troublesome Welsh rulers once and for all and impose stability.

In the eleventh and twelfth centuries English kings led a number of military campaigns in Wales but not one of them, from William the Conqueror's march to St David's in 1081 onwards, was undertaken with the aim of conquest. Every one of these campaigns had a specific and limited objective. That of 1081 may have been intended as a display of force to remind the south Wales rulers and particularly Rhys ap Tewdwr of the power of the king of England. William Rufus's two abortive expeditions in 1095 and 1097 were intended to put an end to the war in north Wales, while the purpose of the two campaigns of Henry I in 1114 and 1121 was to fire a warning shot across the bows of Gruffydd ap Cynan on the first occasion and Maredudd ap Bleddyn on the second. Henry II's campaign of 1157 was a response to the eastward advance of Owain Gwynedd and the consequent appearance of Welsh power on the very outskirts of Chester; his campaigns against Rhys ap Gruffydd were aimed at securing a measure of stability in south Wales where Rhys, the last surviving son of Gruffydd ap Rhys, was something of a wild card.

Henry's campaign of 1164 was carefully planned.He came to terms with potential opponents on the continent and hired mercenaries, as well as a fleet from Dublin. Faced with this threat the Welsh rulers came together under Owain Gwynedd's leadership to resist; an army was organised and assembled in the valley of the Dee at Corwen. In July 1165 Henry set out from Oswestry with the intention of crossing the Berwyn mountains and descending into the Dee valley. The enterprise was a complete fiasco; Henry's army was driven back by summer storms as it tried to make its way across the mountains and the Welsh won a major victory without striking a blow. It was not the last time that the weather was to be on their side. The episode also shows that Welsh military resistance could involve a great deal more than guerilla warfare; Owain Gwynedd was fully prepared to meet a royal army in the field as he had been in 1157 when he had assembled his army near Hawarden to face Henry's invasion.

The failure of his expedition made it clear to Henry that the military option was not a practical proposition and that there was no way in which he could permanently impose his will on the Welsh by force. He attempted no more invasions; instead he gradually built up a close and friendly personal relationship with Rhys ap Gruffydd, the leading Welsh ruler after the death of Owain Gwynedd in 1170. Henry needed to reappraise his position; the murder of Thomas Becket in 1170 had left him isolated and in 1169 had come the Anglo-Norman invasion of Ireland, most of the leaders of which came from south-west Wales. This new Norman settlement caused Henry some concern since some of its leaders now had a new power-base beyond his control and this may have led him to reconsider his relationship with Rhys. In 1171 he crossed to Ireland to impose his authority on the Normans there and to set on foot what was to be the long and tragic chronicle of Anglo-Irish relations. On his way through south Wales he met Rhys twice; Rhys handed over hostages and a tribute of horses and cattle and on his return Henry met him again at Laugharne and appointed him justiciar or royal representative in south Wales.[26] This meant the delegation to him of any authority which the king might have claimed over his fellow Welsh rulers; it might also have involved some authority over the king's Anglo-Norman subjects. Rhys was now both a Welsh king ruling in his hereditary lands and the king of England's representative and the result was peace for the rest of Henry's reign. Rhys was more than a native Welsh ruler; he was one of the great feudatories of the Angevin empire.

This personal relationship ensured stability. Potential crises could be defused, as in 1176 when William de Braose murdered several of the leading Welshmen of northern Gwent at Abergavenny. Rhys sent one of his own sons to aid Henry when his sons rebelled in 1173 and in 1175 he led some of the southern rulers to Gloucester to make their peace with the king. At Oxford in 1177 Rhys and Dafydd ab Owain Gwynedd did homage; the fact that they were the only Welsh rulers to do so reflects a polarisation of political power in Wales around Deheubarth and Gwynedd.[27] But the relationship was a personal one; there was no kind of formal structure to sustain it and when Henry died in 1189 it came to an end. Equilibrium was possible, but to endure it needed some kind of institutional structure to support it. On Henry's death war broke out, probably as a result of the new king Richard I's insensitive handling of Rhys, who was himself faced with problems as his sons grew to manhood and became restless.

Norman Influences

The twelfth century saw a measure of native Welsh recovery and revival. Wales was fortunate in having such rulers as Rhys, Owain Gwynedd and Madog ap Maredudd of Powys (d. 1160); these were shrewd men who were able to deal with Henry II on equal terms. This period saw the beginning of one of the great periods of Welsh poetry, the age of the court poets known as the Poets of the Princes, poets like Cynddelw in Powys and Llywarch ap Llywelyn (Prydydd y Moch) in Gwynedd.[28] The relationship of court poet and ruler was something more than that of client and patron; it was the poet, rather than any cleric, who was the ruler's conscience and he might rebuke as well as praise. The legal revival of the twelfth century also had its impact on Wales; the codification of native law, attributed to Hywel Dda, may have come about in Deheubarth under the influence of Rhys ap Gruffydd or the Lord Rhys, as he was generally known. The anonymous biographer of Gruffydd ap Cynan described the latter part of his reign as a period during which Gruffydd made his kingdom 'glitter with lime-washed churches like the firmament with stars'; church-building is usually an indicator of peace and prosperity and in Anglesey in particular there is no lack of twelfth-century work.[29] There is also evidence that increasing population led to the expansion of settlement.

There can be no doubt that the Normans had a significant impact on Wales; they were one of the most important influences and the channel through which many new ideas came. There was certainly an element of conquest and some ambitious Norman adventurers sought to remove Welsh rulers and often succeeded. The creation of the march did not, in itself, bring about any revolutionary change, since the new Norman lord took over and exploited a going concern, but both sides learned from each other. Norman lords acquired many of the characteristics of Welsh kingship because this was the political culture of which they had become a part. The Welsh, for their part, learned military lessons. The Normans introduced castles; in 1093 Rhys ap Tewdwr was killed attacking one at Brecon but the techniques of siegecraft were soon learned. The next step was the building of castles by native rulers; Cadwgan ap Bleddyn of Powys was planning the construction of a castle at Welshpool when he was murdered in 1111 and in 1116 one was built by a local ruler at Cymer near Dolgellau, to be followed by many others.[30] These were motte-and-bailey structures with timber buildings and many of these mottes are still to be seen. From the late twelfth century masonry castles like Dolwyddelan at the head of the Conwy valley began to make their appearance and were frequently used as royal seats. The Welsh were learning the techniques of contemporary warfare and were able to hold their own, and one result was the development of a new kind of military service. Since the tenth century Welsh rulers had tended to use mercenaries, often Hiberno-Norsemen recruited in Dublin, for their own wars. Military service was one of the privileges of the free Welshman but it was limited to 40 days in the year; mercenaries had provided one solution but even before the fall of Dublin to the Normans in 1170 the supply was less certain and the ultimate result was the grant of bond townships to certain free men in return for military service; these grants also involved the delegation of authority over the bondmen resident in these townships.[31] With these changes came changes in military technology, involving not only the castle but also the armoured knight.

Cultural influences worked both ways; a key part may have been played here by the professional interpreters who performed an essential function in the new marcher lordships, providing a channel of communication between the lords and their Welsh subjects. It may have been through them that the Arthurian tradition reached continental Europe, with far-reaching effects on European literature over the centuries.[32] In the same way the Matter of France and French romances may have come to Wales and been translated. In 1176 an *eisteddfod* or competitive gathering of poets and minstrels was held by the Lord Rhys at his new castle at Cardigan; this was the first recorded meeting of its kind and it is usually seen, not entirely accurately, as the ancestor of the modern *eisteddfod*. It is not impossible that the idea for this gathering came from those assemblies of poets and minstrels in south-western France held under the patronage of Henry II's queen Eleanor of Aquitaine; if so, this is another example of the cosmopolitan world of which the Lord Rhys was a part and it could be that the National Eisteddfod of today owes something to the troubadours of the twelfth century.[33] However, Anglo-Norman lords did not become the patrons of the native poetic tradition in Wales in the way that they did in Ireland; possibly they were too close to England.

The relationship between the two peoples was a complex one. It was certainly not one of unremitting hostility; hostility there undoubtedly was, but it usually stemmed from land rather than from race, although the Welsh scholar Rhygyfarch ap Sulien at the end of the eleventh century composed a Latin poem in which he bewailed the havoc wrought by the Normans.[34] The values of the two peoples were not dissimilar; they were warrior aristocracies who respected each other even as they fought. The relationship is symbolised by Gerald of Wales, the grandson of Gerald of Windsor and great-grandson of Rhys ap Tewdwr; he represented the new Cambro-Norman aristocracy which had emerged in Dyfed and which went on to conquer new worlds in Ireland. An anecdote of Gerald's is significant; he recounts the feudal courtesies exchanged at Hereford in 1186 by the Lord Rhys and members of the de Clare family who had for a time conquered Ceredigion.[35] Rhys was a feudal magnate as well as a Welsh prince and other native rulers were similarly influenced. Dafydd, the son and eventual successor of Owain Gwynedd, married Emma of Anjou, the illegitimate half-sister of Henry II, and there was much intermarrying between Welsh dynasties and marcher houses. The eldest legitimate son of the Lord Rhys married a de Braose, a member of what was by then the greatest family in the march. There were atrocities like the slaughter at Abergavenny in 1176, but Welsh–Norman relations were not an unrelieved picture of hostility and oppression. To maintain equilibrium the crown needed both Welsh rulers and Anglo-Norman lords.

The Welsh Church

The Normans had a significant impact on the Welsh church. By 1100 the church in the Celtic parts of Europe was old-fashioned in comparison with the rest of western Christendom. The concept of a 'Celtic church' has long ago earned a decent burial; the church in the Celtic world was an integral part of the western church but its organisation and its usages must have presented an unfamiliar picture to the Normans.[36] It was a world of bishops without cathedrals, of dioceses based on the units of secular authority and waxing and waning with them, and of hereditary abbots. There was some tradition of scholarship, for example at St David's and at Llanbadarn Fawr, associated with Bishop Sulien and his sons, but the Welsh church cannot be described as a power-house of spiritual activity. The Normans were very much associated with the contemporary climate of reform in the western church and with such a background it was hardly surprising that those who came to Wales experienced a culture shock when they came face to face with some of the traditional ecclesiastical usages there, although they were able to live easily enough with them in the early days. But changes soon came. Before long the Normans had introduced mainstream European monasticism in the shape of the order of St Benedict. Small communities were established in newly conquered areas, usually as cells of houses in England or Normandy with which the invaders' families were already associated. Brecon priory, for example, was a cell of Battle. The lands of some old-established Welsh communities were also granted to English houses; those of Llanbadarn Fawr near Aberystwyth were given to the abbey of St Peter at Gloucester by Gilbert fitz Richard some time between 1115 and 1130.[37] It should be added that the Benedictines were not necessarily brought into Wales out of any hostility to the native monastic tradition; they were a response to the practical pastoral problems posed by two different cultures.

Nevertheless the Benedictines were associated with the Norman invader and they cannot be said to have caught the Welsh imagination. The rule of St Benedict was essentially moderate, providing a monastic life for fallible men; the Celtic tradition, on the other hand, stressed a quest for spiritual perfection, although by the twelfth century this was usually honoured more in the breach than in the observance. The order which did evoke a response in the Welsh was that of the Cistercians, who emphasised solitude, austerity and hard manual work. The first community in Wales was at Tintern in Gwent, founded by Normans in 1131, but in 1140 a group of monks from Clairvaux settled at Whitland in the south-west. From there the order spread through the country and a house was eventually established in every Welsh kingdom of any importance.[38] Native rulers were generous with grants of land, especially of extensive tracts of upland pasture, since the monks deliberately avoided centres of population. The order played a prominent part in the history of Wales and such names as Strata Florida, Aberconwy and Neath recur in the historical record. These abbeys became centres of scholarship and of economic life; it was the Cistercians who pioneered large-scale sheep-farming, wool production and coal-mining. And they struck a chord in the Welsh imagination; the austerity of their life was a reminder of the Celtic tradition. In the words of Sir John Lloyd, 'the Cistercian abbot was a St David or a St Teilo restored to life'.[39]

The coming of European monasticism also had its impact on surviving Celtic communities. In Gwynedd several had been reorganised as houses of Augustinian canons by 1250.[40] In the church as a whole territorial dioceses with fixed boundaries emerged, Llandaff in 1107, St David's with the election of the Norman Bernard as its bishop in 1115 and Bangor with the election of David the Scot (in point of fact a Welshman) in 1120. These were followed by further territorial definition, including archdeaconries and rural deaneries and, eventually, parishes. With the new dioceses came the building of cathedrals. The pre-Norman Welsh church had not had the clear-cut chain of command which existed elsewhere; the concept of an archbishop with metropolitan authority was entirely new and as a result the archbishop of Canterbury was able to extend his jurisdiction over Wales. From 1107 every Welsh bishop had to take an oath of canonical obedience to Canterbury before being consecrated and this continued until 1920. But reform never reached most of the parochial clergy and relics of an earlier pattern survived.

Gerald of Wales

The most famous Cambro-Norman was undoubtedly Gerald of Wales. Gerald was born at Manorbier in Dyfed in about 1145 or 1146, the son of William de Barry and his wife Angharad, the daughter of Gerald of Windsor, and he became one of the most distinguished scholars of his time. In the history of Wales he stands out for two reasons: his long battle for the bishopric of St David's and his writings about Wales. There were two issues at stake in the battle for St David's; the immediate one was the acceptability of Gerald as bishop, but the second had wider implications. This was the question of the Welsh church as a distinct ecclesiastical province with its own metropolitan, a matter which had been raised earlier in the century by Bernard, the first Norman bishop of St David's.[41] Bernard was familiar with ecclesiastical practice elsewhere; this was that each nation should have its own metropolitan, subject to the supreme authority of Rome. He had further argued that there should be an archbishop of St David's and that the Welsh church should be entirely independent of Canterbury. He had died before the pope had ruled on the matter and his successor was forced by Canterbury to swear an oath not to raise it again. Gerald had expected to succeed his uncle David fitz Gerald in the see when the latter died in 1176, but his election was vetoed by Henry II who felt that he was too closely related to leading local families, not only in Dyfed but also in Ireland. In 1198 the see was vacant once more and Gerald was once again the obvious candidate. He was elected by the chapter but the election was bitterly opposed by Hubert Walter, the archbishop of Canterbury, who was well-aware of the potential implications of Gerald's success. There was a long struggle which involved several visits by Gerald to Rome to plead his case before the pope, Innocent III. Innocent was sympathetic but in the end Gerald had to concede defeat and Wales had to wait until the twentieth century for its own archbishop. He retired to Lincoln to his beloved books and there he died in 1223. The crown, with its massive resources, had proved too powerful for him and his own sharp tongue and caustic wit had made him many enemies. But the battle was an important one in the history of the Welsh church and it is well-documented in Gerald's voluminous writings.[42]

It is by his writings about Wales that Gerald is mainly remembered. He was one of the most prolific authors of his time; he wrote, for example, two books about Ireland, where he had spent some time and where he had many kinsmen. In 1188 Baldwin, the archbishop of Canterbury, visited Wales, ostensibly to preach the Third Crusade; the real object, however, was to demonstrate the authority of Canterbury by celebrating mass in each of the four Welsh cathedrals.[43] Gerald accompanied the archbishop and his account of the journey is a graphic picture of Wales at the end of the twelfth century, with many entertaining digressions, anecdotes and descriptions of signs and wonders which reflect the credulity that could go with the sophistication of a twelfth-century intellectual. His second book on Wales, the *Description*, is more objective but has to be treated with some caution as a source for contemporary Welsh life.[44] Gerald was not always as well-informed about Wales as he thought and it has recently been suggested that the book was based more on the pattern of contemporary ethnographic writing about the remoter peoples of Europe than on his own direct observation.[45] The book is set out like the kind of scholastic exercise with which Gerald was familiar; the first part deals with the virtues of the Welsh and the second with their faults. Gerald of Wales was the creature of his age and cultural background. His mother tongue was Norman French and he probably had no more than a smattering of Welsh; in adult life his main language would have been Latin. Canonist, churchman, administrator, academic and gossip, there were many like him in the twelfth century but Gerald reveals more of himself than most. He was disappointed in his ambition but the St David's issue became a national one and some see him as an important figure in the development of Welsh national awareness.[46]

3

THE AGE OF THE PRINCES

Llywelyn ab Iorwerth

By 1200 Gwynedd was finally emerging as the undisputed leader in Wales. Powys had enjoyed a period of strength in the mid-twelfth century under Madog ap Maredudd but Madog had died in 1160 and his son and designated heir Llywelyn had been killed soon afterwards. The kingdom was divided, the north going to another of Madog's sons and the south to his nephew Owain Cyfeiliog; the division was permanent and Powys ceased to be one of the major powers in Wales. It had never been easy for it to pursue an independent policy, sandwiched as it was between Gwynedd and England, and its rulers had generally seen the English crown as a bulwark against the expansionist ambitions of Gwynedd. On the death of Owain Gwynedd in 1170 the Lord Rhys had taken his place as the dominant ruler in Wales, but the supremacy of Deheubarth was short-lived. The kingdom had not been created until the early tenth century and loyalties therefore tended to be to its component parts. Rhys seems to have striven to create a distinct Deheubarth identity, involving the encouragement of a cult of Hywel Dda as the founder of the kingdom, but it was probably only his personality that held it together. It was a far more fissiparous political unit than Gwynedd or Powys; Gwyn A. Williams has described it very appropriately as a 'ramshackle confederation'.[1] When Rhys died in 1197 it fell apart; his son Gruffydd was the designated heir but he was challenged by an older brother Maelgwn, born out of wedlock but legitimate in Welsh eyes. The power struggle was never resolved; Deheubarth was never reassembled and the descendants of Rhys's sons went their separate ways.

Owain Gwynedd had many sons by different mothers; his chosen successor was probably Hywel, a poet of some distinction, but his succession was disputed by two of his half-brothers, Dafydd and Rhodri, who were far younger than him. Soon after Owain's death Hywel was killed in battle and a fight for power, involving most of the surviving brothers, followed. The ultimate result was the division of Gwynedd, the east and the kingship going to Dafydd, the west to Rhodri and the south to the sons of another brother, Cynan. For the next few years there was some sort of equilibrium, although there is actually very little surviving information about Gwynedd during this period. By the last decade of the century, however, a new force had emerged. This was Llywelyn ab Iorwerth, the son of Iorwerth Drwyndwn (Broken-nose), possibly the eldest legitimate son of Owain Gwynedd, who is said to have been excluded from the succession because of a physical disability.[2] Llywelyn began to challenge his uncles at a very early age and eventually drove them both out.[3] By 1200 most of Gwynedd was under his direct control and he was well on the way to becoming the predominant power in Wales. He had, however, to face opposition from Powys. Owain Cyfeiliog had died in 1197 and had been succeeded by his son Gwenwynwyn who, despite the division of the kingdom in 1160, had political ambitions beyond its borders; the ensuing struggle took up much of the first decade of the thirteenth century. From 1199 John, Henry II's youngest son, had been king of England and he probably understood Welsh politics better than any English king before or since, having himself been lord of Glamorgan in right of his first wife. John was able to play the two Welsh rulers off against each other, sometimes favouring Llywelyn and sometimes Gwenwynwyn. In 1201 Llywelyn and John made a treaty, the first formal written agreement between a Welsh ruler and a king of England.[4] When Gwenwynwyn fell from favour with the king in 1208 Llywelyn marched into southern Powys. At the time he was in favour; in 1204 he had married the king's illegitimate daughter Joan and this marriage was a sign that Gwynedd had now drawn ahead of the other Welsh kingdoms. A Plantagenet marriage, even with an illegitimate daughter, would bring with it dynastic links that would, in the long term, elevate the status of the house of Gwynedd. The children that Joan would bear Llywelyn would be the descendants of Henry II, Eleanor of Aquitaine, Malcolm Canmore and the counts of Anjou.

The marriage was a political success; Joan was a great help to Llywelyn in his dealings with his father-in-law and relations began well. In 1209 Llywelyn joined John on his campaign in Scotland, one of the few recorded occasions when a Welsh prince joined an English king on a military expedition outside Wales.[5] But John may have become alarmed by Llywelyn's growing power and he may have played on the jealousy and suspicion of the other Welsh rulers. In 1211 he invaded Gwynedd and in a lightning campaign he burned the town of Bangor and kidnapped the bishop. Llywelyn was forced to submit, to cede north-east Wales, to hand over hostages, including his son Gruffydd, and to pay a heavy tribute of cattle.[6] John went too far, however, when he showed every sign of staying in Wales and began to build castles. The other rulers, who had hitherto been his allies, were alarmed and made their peace with Llywelyn and the situation changed overnight. The king was planning a major campaign in France to recover Normandy and Anjou, lost to the French in 1204. At the same time Llywelyn was planning a renewal of hostilities and he and the other rulers, particularly Gwenwynwyn in Powys and Maelgwn ap Rhys in Deheubarth, had the support of the pope, Innocent III, who had long been in dispute with John. Innocent released Wales from the interdict which had followed the beginning of that dispute and it may have been at his instigation that Llywelyn in 1212 made a treaty on behalf of himself and the other Welsh rulers with Philip Augustus of France.[7] John was unable to retaliate; a planned campaign in Wales had to be abandoned and in 1213 Llywelyn reconquered the north-east. In 1214 John's ally, the German emperor Otto IV, suffered a crushing defeat at the hands of the French at Bouvines; this marked the complete collapse of his foreign policy and the following year he was forced by the baronial opposition in England to grant Magna Carta.

The Charter obliged John to release the Welsh hostages and to return the charters extorted from Welsh rulers in 1211.[8] For Llywelyn, who had supported the baronial party, a successful campaign in south Wales was followed by an assembly of rulers at Aberdyfi in 1216 when reconquered territory was shared out among members of the Deheubarth dynasty and where the other lords may have done him homage.[9] In the same year Gwenwynwyn changed sides and was driven out of Powys to die in exile in England soon afterwards; there was no room in Wales for two ambitious rulers. At the same time Llywelyn maintained good relations with his marcher neighbours and with the most powerful magnate on the border, the earl of Chester; his four daughters and his heir all married into Anglo-Norman marcher families, one daughter marrying the earl of Chester's heir. These marriages were aimed at building up the position of Gwynedd and developing dynastic links with the march, possibly with the long-term view of creating ties of dependence. A new line of policy was now taking shape in Gwynedd, its object being the unification of native Wales by the development of a feudal relationship. Other rulers would be persuaded or forced to do homage to the prince of Gwynedd who would become their overlord; they had previously done it directly to the king of England. The prince would now do homage to the king on behalf of the other rulers and would thus become the conduit of their homage or, as Sir Maurice Powicke put it, 'the keystone in an arch of kings'.[10] Thus a single Welsh principality would at last be able to develop.

John's death in 1216 was followed in England by the minority of his son Henry III and by civil war. This ended with the Treaty of Lambeth in 1217; Llywelyn was not a party to this but the Peace of Worcester of 1218 confirmed his territorial gains and brought hostilities to an end.[11] This was followed by a period of relative peace in Anglo-Welsh relations but in the mid-1220s the prince was faced with a struggle with the young king's regent Hubert de Burgh who was ambitious to build up a powerful lordship for himself in the march and who in 1224 built a large new castle for the king at Montgomery. Llywelyn was, however, able to contain Hubert's activities and the Pact of Myddle of 1234 secured a truce which lasted until his death, although this was not achieved without further military campaigns in 1231 and 1233.[12] He was now the undisputed ruler of native Wales and in 1230 he adopted a new title, prince of Aberffraw and lord of Snowdon; he had previously styled himself prince of North Wales. The new title reflected the basis of his power and authority in Gwynedd and stressed its history by associating his supremacy with the traditional seat of the kingship of Gwynedd at Aberffraw in Anglesey. Welsh rulers had by now ceased to call themselves kings, a change which may have been the consequence of a more precise definition of kingship in twelfth-century Europe. Owain Gwynedd had at different times styled himself both king and prince of Wales and of the Welsh, while his son Dafydd came to call himself prince of north Wales; the Lord Rhys had used 'prince of Wales', 'prince of the Welsh' and 'prince of south Wales'.[13]

From about 1220 one of Llywelyn's prime objectives was to secure the undivided succession of one heir and thus avoid the division of the inheritance. He had two sons, Gruffydd by an early marriage or liaison and Dafydd by Joan. Dafydd was chosen as the heir; it was, in political and dynastic terms, a logical choice since Dafydd was the nephew of Henry III and had genuine and undisputed royal blood in his veins. His father took steps to have him recognised as the designated heir by the other Welsh rulers, the king and the papacy, in order to settle the question of the succession during his own lifetime.[14] Gruffydd was excluded from the succession but Llywelyn's intention was to give him a substantial appanage; at one time he held Powys. He was, however, resentful and rebelled against his father on more than one occasion; at the time of Llywelyn's death he and his eldest son Owain were prisoners in Cricieth castle. A marriage was arranged for Dafydd with a daughter of the leading marcher magnate, William de Braose, who had earlier been Llywelyn's prisoner. During his captivity de Braose had had an affair with Joan and on his return to the prince's court in 1230 to discuss the arrangements for the marriage the couple were caught by the prince in Joan's chamber. De Braose was hanged but the marriage went ahead and there were no repercussions; the de Braose family was far from popular and it may have been generally felt that William had betrayed the laws of hospitality.

Llywelyn needed more than the acceptance of Dafydd as his successor. The vision which he and his advisers had of a new Welsh principality needed one thing to become a reality; this was recognition by the English crown, enshrined in a formal treaty. This was Llywelyn's objective for the rest of his reign and his diplomatic activity was geared to it. Henry III understood very well what the prince was trying to do and was not prepared to accept it; he had to accept Llywelyn's own position but he had no wish to see it inherited by his successor. A treaty would give a Welsh principality a secure institutional and constitutional basis and would make permanent the office of prince of Wales; Llywelyn may have chosen deliberately not to adopt this title pending a treaty. The king's long-term aim was to regain the direct overlordship of every Welsh ruler and he would not enter into any commitment which would bind him after Llywelyn's death.

1237 was a fateful year for Llywelyn ab Iorwerth. It saw the deaths of Joan, long reconciled with her husband, and of his son-in-law the earl of Chester, an event which brought Chester into the possession of the crown and therefore affected the position on his eastern border. In addition to this, he suffered a stroke and, although he recovered, Dafydd seems to have become the effective ruler. In April 1240 he died and was buried in the abbey of Aberconwy. He was one of the greatest of all Welsh rulers and is remembered as Llywelyn Fawr, Llywelyn the Great; the title seems first to have been used by the English chronicler Matthew Paris.[15] On the face of it he appeared to have created a strong principality, but on his death its underlying weaknesses were made manifest. The disinheriting of his eldest son was seen by some in Wales as a breach with tradition. In 1238 he had summoned the other rulers to the Cistercian abbey of Strata Florida to do homage to Dafydd; the ceremony may have been intended to mark his effective abdication and the investiture of Dafydd as the next prince. But when Henry III heard what was planned he wrote to the other rulers, forbidding them to do homage; this suggests that he knew very well what Llywelyn was trying to do and would not permit it. He could do nothing about Llywelyn himself but under no circumstances would he allow his successor to occupy a similar position. Henry's response pinpointed Llywelyn's weakness; everything that he had built up had depended on his personality and his own strength. As long as he lived his principality was safe but there was no institutional framework to sustain it once he was gone. A treaty would have secured it, but Henry knew this as well as he did, which explains why the two rulers never reached the conference table.

Dafydd ap Llywelyn

Henry's attitude was made very clear on Llywelyn's death. Within a month Dafydd was summoned to meet the king at Gloucester. He was knighted and a treaty was concluded, but it was nothing like the treaty which Llywelyn had sought.[16] Under its terms all Welsh rulers were in future to do homage directly to the king. Dafydd did homage but so did all the other lords; it was a public humiliation and Henry was able to take advantage of the pent-up resentment of the other rulers after Llywelyn's reign. Llywelyn's principality had been dismantled at one stroke. On his return home Dafydd tried to ignore the provisions of the treaty and to procrastinate; Henry's response was an invasion of north Wales in 1241, as a result of which Dafydd was forced to accept the Treaty of Gwern Eigron under which he had to surrender all his father's territorial gains, cede the cantref of Englefield (the later Flintshire) to the crown and hand his brother Gruffydd over to the king.[17] In the Treaty of London a few months later he agreed that Gwynedd would escheat to the crown if he died without direct heirs.[18] Gruffydd merely moved from one captivity to another; he was far too valuable a bargaining counter to be set free and he was safely lodged in the Tower of London as the king's honoured guest.

Dafydd was in a difficult position. He had to tread very carefully because he knew very well that one false step would bring a royal army to Gwynedd to install Gruffydd in his place. The king was anxious to divide what remained of Llywelyn's principality between the two brothers through an action in his court. But on 1 March 1244 Dafydd was relieved of one of his problems. Gruffydd was killed in an attempt to escape from the Tower and Henry III lost a valuable hostage. In the same year Dafydd attempted to place Gwynedd under papal overlordship; this was a not uncommon course of action by small kingdoms and principalities threatened by powerful neighbours. It had been done at different times by Portugal, Denmark and the Manx kingdom and John had done it in England in 1213 when threatened by the baronial party.[19] Dafydd's bid, however, was unsuccessful; when Henry III heard of it he paid off the arrears of the tribute which John had agreed to pay but which had long been ignored and used his influence at Rome. The pope needed the support and goodwill of the king of England in his struggle with the house of Hohenstaufen but Dafydd could offer no such political dividend. Around the same time Dafydd had begun to style himself prince of Wales, the first use of the title in the thirteenth century; this may have been connected with his bid for papal protection, implying a rejection of that overlordship of the English crown which had been accepted by Welsh rulers for several centuries.[20] War was renewed in 1245 but in February 1246 Dafydd died, leaving no children. His position had been weakened by Gruffydd's supporters and because of this his reign has often been seen as no more than a stopgap between the two Llywelyns; however, he seized every possible opportunity and Sir John Lloyd's description of his reign as 'an unfinished experiment' is probably a fair judgement.[21]

Llywelyn ap Gruffydd

Gwynedd was now faced with a succession problem. Gruffydd ap Llywelyn had four sons, Owain, Llywelyn, Dafydd and Rhodri. Llywelyn was in Gwynedd and seems by 1246 to have given his support to his uncle, making him the natural successor; Owain, the eldest brother, rushed to Gwynedd to stake his claim but, faced with a renewed royal campaign, the two brothers were persuaded to divide Gwynedd between them. Their position was particularly weak; the royal armies were closing in and things were made worse by famine. They had to come to terms and the Treaty of Woodstock at the end of April 1247 was the result.[22] This was the nadir of Welsh fortunes before 1282 and its conditions were particularly humiliating. The brothers had to agree to hold their lands of the crown in chief by military service; in other words they had to accept a position similar to that of English tenants-in-chief, rather than that of sovereign rulers whose authority did not derive from the crown. They had also to agree that Gwynedd would escheat to the crown if they both died without direct heirs, a repetition of the terms of the Treaty of London, and the settlement included the cession of the Four Cantrefs, the territory between the Conwy and the Dee. Woodstock could be described as a kind of creeping annexation of Gwynedd by Henry III. There was no legal basis whatsoever for the terms he imposed; he was taking full advantage of temporary weakness and in the long term the provisions of the treaty were probably unenforceable. However, the sequence of Anglo-Welsh treaties of the 1240s does indicate the political skill of Henry III and suggests that he has, in some respects, been underrated by historians. Gloucester, Gwern Eigron, London and Woodstock reflect an understanding of the dynamics of Welsh dynastic and territorial politics and a coherent policy towards Wales based on the premise that never again would a ruler like Llywelyn ab Iorwerth be permitted to emerge.

Henry could not maintain this dominance; as his position was weakened by growing political opposition in England, Owain and Llywelyn began to recover theirs. Agreements were made with other Welsh rulers, although Henry was now pressing for a further division of Gwynedd to provide for the third brother, Dafydd.[23] Before there could be much progress, one matter had to be resolved; there was no room for two princes. Things came to a head in 1255 when Owain and Dafydd, who was by now his *penteulu* or military commander, were defeated by Llywelyn in the battle of Bryn Derwin. Owain's fate was to be imprisoned for the next 22 years; several poets were to rebuke Llywelyn for his treatment of his elder brother but he really had little choice.[24] Owain was a man of ability and free he would always have been a threat. Brothers could be a menace in the Welsh political world and Llywelyn was bound to remember the experience of his uncle with his father. After Bryn Derwin he was in sole control of Gwynedd but he had now to consolidate his position. Owain had had his supporters and they had to be conciliated.

By 1256 Llywelyn was able to move. In 1254 the Four Cantrefs had been granted by Henry III to his eldest son, the Lord Edward. Edward's officials soon gained a bad reputation for insensitive and extortionate rule. The people of the Four Cantrefs appealed to Llywelyn for help and in the autumn of 1256 he crossed the Conwy. Within a week the whole of the Four Cantrefs, apart from two castles, was in his hands. This was followed by two years of successful campaigning all over Wales, which brought Meirionnydd, Deheubarth and Powys either under his overlordship or his direct control. In 1257 a royal army was defeated at Cymerau near Carmarthen by some of the Deheubarth lords and a planned royal campaign in north Wales was a total failure. By 1258 every Welsh ruler except Gruffydd ap Gwenwynwyn of southern Powys was on Llywelyn's side; in this year they all seem to have done homage to him and from now on he was calling himself prince of Wales.[25] A treaty was made by all the Welsh lords, led by the prince, with a faction of Scottish lords against Henry III; it did not lead to anything but it does show one possible line of development if things had turned out differently.[26] The early 1260s saw further successful campaigns and territorial gains. Having established his control over those parts of Wales which were under native rule,

Llywelyn now moved into parts of the march. He was now in control of the strategic heartland of Wales; another planned royal campaign was abortive and by the end of 1263 even Gruffydd ap Gwenwynwyn, under pressure from some of his marcher neighbours, had made his peace, although the prince's brother Dafydd changed sides in the same year.[27] The English crown no longer posed a threat; the growing tension between the king and the baronial party under Simon de Montfort led in 1264 to the outbreak of civil war. Llywelyn and Simon were natural allies, especially after the latter's victory at Lewes in 1264 when Henry III and Edward were captured. Edward's escape and the change of allegiance of the earl of Gloucester, the last remaining baronial supporter in the march, strengthened the prince's position immensely, since he was now Simon's only ally and could dictate his own terms. The result, in June 1265, was the Treaty of Pipton in which Simon promised in the king's name to recognise Llywelyn as prince of Wales and overlord of the other Welsh rulers; Llywelyn agreed to pay £20,000 over a period of ten years and to do homage to the king.[28]

The terms agreed at Pipton are important. It is very easy to see Llywelyn ap Gruffydd as a romantic figure and patriotic hero, winning battles and imposing his will on the English and on his fellow-rulers. There is no doubt that he was an outstanding military commander and charismatic leader; one English chronicler commented that the Welsh followed him as if they were glued to him.[29] Mobility was the secret of much of his military success; he could move an army from one end of Wales to the other very rapidly, using upland routes, and he was a master of surprise. But there was more to him than that. He was a shrewd politician who understood very well that military victory was not enough and that the gains which it brought might very well only be temporary. The only way to secure his principality was by the treaty which his grandfather had sought in vain and this had to be bought as well as agreed. He had been seeking such a treaty for some time but he had to negotiate from a position of strength. He was ready to discuss a settlement in 1259 when he offered £3,000 for a treaty; he made a further offer of £16,000 the same year but there was no response from Henry.[30] The sums he was prepared to offer show how anxious he was to establish Anglo-Welsh relations on a formal footing.

The Pipton agreement never took effect. Simon de Montfort's fate was probably already sealed by then and two months later he was defeated and killed by Edward at Evesham. Llywelyn knew perfectly well that Simon was in no position to offer an enduring settlement; for him Pipton was a marker, setting out the terms he was seeking from the crown. Evesham really marked the end of the civil war; both sides wanted reconciliation and the papal representative Ottobuono came to England to act as mediator. Talks, brokered by Ottobuono, were held between Llywelyn's representatives and those of the crown and the result, on 29 September 1267, was the Treaty of Montgomery.[31]

The Treaty of Montgomery was the high point of achievement for the princes of Gwynedd; in it Llywelyn secured everything for which three successive princes had worked. He was recognised as prince of Wales and overlord of all the other Welsh rulers; more importantly, his successors would also be recognised. His territorial gains, including the key border areas which he had to control if his principality was to have any credibility, were confirmed. He was reconciled with his brother Dafydd. For all this he did homage and agreed to pay 25,000 marks (£16,667) in ten annual instalments. What this treaty meant was that in future there would be a principality of Wales, recognised by the English crown as a constitutional entity. The prince would do homage to the king of England and the other Welsh lords would do homage to him. There was for the first time a stable relationship, based on a formal agreement enshrined in a treaty agreed by both sides. This was what Llywelyn ab Iorwerth had sought throughout the 1230s but he had never been able to achieve it. Llywelyn ap Gruffydd had learned from the fate of his grandfather's principality in 1240; he and his advisers realised that a formal institutional framework was the only way to secure the principality for the future. His life's work could not be allowed to evaporate because of the death of one man; the permanence of the office of prince would ensure the survival of the principality.

Change in the Thirteenth Century

1267 is an appropriate date at which to pause and examine the ways in which thirteenth-century Wales was changing. In Gwynedd much of this change was the result of the policies of the princes who realised that a Welsh principality had to be something more than a collection of homages. The key to much of this change lies in the law. Welsh law, the law of Hywel Dda, was not static; it developed and changed to meet the changing needs of society. The revival of interest in legal studies which was so pronounced a feature of twelfth-century Europe had not passed Wales by and the lawbooks which survive from the thirteenth century contain a great deal of evidence of legal change. Most of these texts were probably prepared by practising lawyers, either for their own use or as textbooks for students. In Gwynedd there were professional judges and lawyers, although in other parts of Wales the courts tended to be communal institutions, and some of the changes were the work of these legal practitioners. The very nature of the new principality had legal implications. The position of the prince had to be built up to make him an effective overlord. Provision had to be made for the feudal obligation of military service; this was included in Gruffydd ap Gwenwynwyn's submission to Llywelyn ap Gruffydd in 1263. The attempt to create a legal basis for the principality can be seen in many ways; where there had been many kings, there was now one prince and the other native rulers were, in effect, his barons or tenants-in-chief. There was therefore a need to devise an entirely new body of law to govern the prince's relations with other rulers. The lawyers were one of the strongest influences for unity, bred, as they were, in a common legal tradition, and leading jurists must have been well-aware of contemporary developments in England and elsewhere.

The new principality and the concomitant expansion of

princely power brought with it the concept of the state. Welsh law was essentially *volksrecht* rather than *kaiserrecht*; in other words it operated as between kindreds or individuals rather than involving the ruler or the state. Even such offences as homicide were treated as offences against the kindred of the victim and not offences against the state; amends were made by the payment of compensation, not by punishment. In thirteenth-century Gwynedd, however, such offences were becoming offences against the prince, who acted as an impartial arbitrator and executioner and who was coming to see doing justice between his people as part of his duty. By the thirteenth century, at least in Gwynedd, the elaborate procedure of *galanas* or compensation for homicide was on the way out. One of the witnesses who appeared before Edward I's commission of enquiry into Welsh legal procedure in 1281 stated that *galanas* had been abolished by Dafydd ap Llywelyn and his council, partly because innocent kinsmen objected to contributing to compensation for an offence in which they had not been involved; this was cited as an example of the power of the prince to change the law.[32] The procedure did, in fact, survive in other parts of Wales and there is no lack of examples; in many cases it came to be replaced by arbitration and there is a case from Gwynedd as late as 1523.[33]

In the prince's high court something like English procedure seems to have been used, although surviving records of lawsuits suggest that the law might very often lie in the will of the prince rather than in the legal text.[34] The choice of procedure might often be determined by which was the more likely to operate to the prince's advantage. Throughout Europe the thirteenth century was the age of the lawyers; they set the tone of an age in which governments were becoming more active, especially in such fields as law and taxation. There was an increasing emphasis on definition and on precise frontiers and administrative units. At the same time the century saw the crystallisation of political ideas, the emergence of theories of lordship and sovereignty and the growth of concepts of national policy which can be seen so clearly in the England of Edward I and the France of Philip the Fair, and in thirteenth-century Wales, too, a sense of national identity, in some ways associated with the law of Hywel Dda, can be seen emerging.

An emergent state needed a bureaucracy. Government was becoming a more complex operation. The law books described an elaborate hierarchy of court officials but by the thirteenth century this section was of mainly antiquarian interest. By now the prince had a writing office which produced his charters and letters and which saw to the keeping of records. He had his great and privy seals; part of the great seal of Llywelyn ab Iorwerth may be seen on his letter of 1212 to Philip Augustus, now in the Archives Nationales in Paris.[35] This seal would be affixed to charters to religious houses and to individuals and to letters to other rulers and magnates. The prince had a small staff of clerks, the names of many of whom are known, but the operations of his government were not so elaborate that there was any degree of specialisation; individual servants dealt with whatever business there was to hand, be it secretarial, financial or diplomatic.[36] The office of *distain* or steward, responsible in the Laws for the domestic management of the court, had developed, probably under the influence of the corresponding office in the march, into the prince's chief adviser and executive official. The best-known holder of this office was Ednyfed Fychan, who held it from about 1215 to his death in 1246 and who was followed in the office by two, possibly three, of his sons; his nephew Goronwy ap Heilin was the last holder of the office and was killed in action in 1283.[37] Ednyfed's descendants played a prominent part in the affairs of Wales during the fourteenth century and one of them became king of England in 1485. These men had to be rewarded; extents and surveys compiled in the fourteenth century reveal extensive grants of land made outside the hereditary pattern, held of the prince by suit of court and military service. Ednyfed Fychan was the best-known recipient of these grants; most of them were in Anglesey, but some were in his native area near Abergele.

The century also saw significant military changes. It had originally been the privilege of every freeman to follow the prince to war. Every ruler also had his *teulu*, his warband or body of household troops, fed and mounted by him, who were expected to die with him if necessary. This primitive pattern of military organisation was geared to raids on the lands of neighbouring kings; the host could only be summoned for service outside the kingdom once a year and then for no more than six weeks. But the large-scale campaigns of Llywelyn ab Iorwerth and Llywelyn ap Gruffydd required a different kind of organisation. The prince now had armoured knights and siege-engines; Llywelyn ab Iorwerth used catapults when besieging Brecon in 1233 and Cnwclas surrendered to Llywelyn ap Gruffydd in 1262 'for fear of the engines'.[38] Llywelyn ap Gruffydd also appears to have had a small fleet which he used in 1257 to cut off royal reinforcements from Ireland.[39] It is possible that there was some attempt to organise the landward defences of Gwynedd, using a combination of geography and castles.[40] The heartland of Snowdonia was protected by controlling the key barrier zones; the location of the castles built by Llywelyn ab Iorwerth suggests both careful planning and the exploitation of geography. Logistic efficiency was the key to successful defence and involved the protection of the main corn-growing areas of Anglesey and Llŷn.

Castles could be used for attack or defence; those of the native princes lack the sophistication of those built later by Edward I but this is a reflection of the resources available to Llywelyn ab Iorwerth. At Dolbadarn near Llanberis in Snowdonia, for example, the cylindrical keep is of good-quality masonry but the adjacent buildings are not of the same standard. There are signs in some castles of outside influences; the Dolbadarn keep may stem from Llywelyn's acquaintance with similar castles built in south-east Wales by Hubert de Burgh, while the gatehouse at Cricieth, the only native coastal castle, bears a strong resemblance to that at Beeston in Cheshire, built by his ally Earl Ranulf III of Chester.[41] There is a significant difference in the siting of native Welsh and Edwardian castles; the former were intended to cover internal lines of communication and as a defence against an external enemy, while the latter were 'the premium Edward paid to insure his Welsh conquests against the fire of rebellion'.[42] Food supplies for the castles were organised by the adaptation of carrying services and by the establishment of vaccaries or cattle farms in their vicinity. The whole defensive system of Gwynedd was geared to defence against invasion from the east; the only way in which it could be countered was by the use of sea-power through seizing the main source of food supplies and bottling the Welsh up in Snowdonia, as Edward I was to do.

With these developments went economic change. The thirteenth century saw the expansion of trade and the wider circulation of money. Rulers had once lived on the food renders delivered by their subjects as they travelled around the kingdom; now these had been replaced by payments in cash, although in Gwynedd renders in kind were still due from unfree communities to maintain the prince and his retinue.[43] Cash was now an essential ingredient of lordship, to pay for the Treaty of Montgomery and to meet the running expenses, political and military, of the new principality. This speeded up the development of a money economy and Llywelyn ap Gruffydd in particular was able to find substantial sums. Thirteenth-century Wales was not rich, but it was far removed from a primitive barter economy.

The growth of trade was also consistent with the military policy of the princes. Small urban settlements were growing up as trading centres, usually on the prince's demesne, and some of these developed into boroughs. At Nefyn in Llŷn as early as the last decade of the twelfth century a grant of bondmen was witnessed by two burgesses of the town; such burgesses might be farmers or fishermen who were also part-time traders.[44] Llanfaes in Anglesey, at the northern end of the Menai Straits, was a flourishing port and market centre with a Franciscan friary founded by Llywelyn ab Iorwerth in memory of his wife and in a post-conquest petition the burgesses of Llan-faes referred to the charters granted to them by the princes.[45] Import duties were levied on ale and wine landed at the port and there was a flourishing herring fishery; two fairs were held each year and wool and hides were exported. It has been suggested that the port handled 70 per cent of the external trade of Gwynedd and post-conquest evidence indicates the existence of some prosperous merchants there. Pwllheli in Llŷn had fairs and income from customs duties and tolls, while at Nefyn in 1292–3 there were 50 free households paying cash rents, including an innkeeper and a goldsmith.[46] Other urban centres in Gwynedd included Caernarfon, Tywyn and Dolgellau in Meirionnydd, Trefriw in the Conwy valley and Llannerch-y-medd in Anglesey. In Powys there were market centres at Machynlleth, Llanfyllin and Llanrhaiadr-ym-Mochnant and in Ceredigion at Lampeter and Trefilan. Towns in Pura Wallia were not post-conquest implantations.

Thirteenth-century Wales was changing; the paradox was that in Gwynedd, under native Welsh rule, the pace of change was far more rapid than it was in many of the marcher lordships where Anglo-Norman lords accepted the system and the profits of lordship as they were, although in such lordships as Glamorgan the position of the lord was becoming much more clearly defined. Native Wales was now far from being a tribal society if, indeed, it ever had been. There was no lack of foreign trade and some wealth. Money was circulating, spurred on by the need of Llywelyn ap Gruffydd for as much ready cash as possible to sustain his principality.

Crises and Conquest

As Llywelyn and his entourage rode home from Montgomery the future of the principality must have seemed secure. Yet, in just over fifteen years, he was dead and what was left of his principality was in the hands of the king of England. Whatever had been secured by the treaty, it was only a beginning. The task facing Llywelyn in 1267 was to make his principality a reality, to create a real monarchy and to make his overlordship of the other rulers permanent; they were proud men whose own ancestors had been kings and they would have to be handled with tact and sensitivity. New institutions had to be created to serve the new principality. The new era in Anglo-Welsh relations had started promisingly enough. Llywelyn paid the instalments due for the treaty on time; by 1272 he had paid a total of 13,750 marks and he had paid a further 5,000 for the homage of one of the Deheubarth lords who had been excluded from the treaty.[47] But it was not long before problems began to arise. Henry III died in 1272 and was succeeded by his son Edward I. Edward was out of the country at the time, being on his way back from the crusade; he did not arrive back in England until 1274, by which time there were already tensions in Anglo-Welsh relations.

The first cause of tension was a dispute between Llywelyn and the earl of Gloucester over the lordship of Glamorgan. This was one of the consequences of the Treaty of Montgomery, under which Llywelyn was recognised as overlord of all the other Welsh lords. Unfortunately the boundaries and territorial extent of his principality had not been defined, but he regarded himself as being entitled to the homage of those Welsh lords who had survived in Glamorgan. In 1268 Gloucester began building a new castle at Caerffili. Llywelyn saw this as a provocation and in 1270, after several fruitless attempts at arbitration, he destroyed the castle. This was followed by a long and inconclusive campaign in the north of the lordship; the prince was eventually forced to withdraw and this was highly significant since it showed that he could be resisted. In 1273 Llywelyn also began building a castle at Dolforwyn in Cydewain in mid-Wales, one of the lordships he had captured, and he established a market nearby. The burgesses of the adjacent town of Montgomery protested and the three regents who were governing the kingdom in Edward's absence ordered him to stop; it was probably significant that one of the regents was Roger Mortimer, who had lost Cydewain to Llywelyn. The prince replied that they had no right to interfere and that he was entitled to build castles in his own principality.[48]

In the same year he had failed to appear to do homage to the new king and he had stopped paying the instalments for the treaty. In 1272 he only paid a quarter of what was due and he subsequently paid nothing; his excuse was that the money would be paid as soon as his grievances were remedied. Thus, by the time Edward returned, relations had already begun to deteriorate. Although summoned to the coronation, Llywelyn failed to attend. Negotiations did begin but in 1274 the prince was faced with a major political and personal crisis. Dafydd, his brother and heir, and Gruffydd ap Gwenwynwyn, the lord of southern Powys, had plotted to assassinate him. The deed had been planned for 2 February 1274 but had been foiled by bad weather; had it succeeded, Dafydd would have become prince and Gruffydd's eldest son and heir Owain would have married his daughter. Llywelyn seems gradually to have become aware of the plot; Gruffydd was put on trial and obliged to ask for pardon, while Dafydd escaped to England before the date set for his interrogation. But it was not until Owain, who had been handed over to the prince as a hostage, made a full confession that Llywelyn learned all the details.[49] Gruffydd fled to join Dafydd in England after imprisoning the delegation sent to his castle at Welshpool to question him. The two plotters were granted asylum by Edward and they carried out several raids on Llywelyn's lands.

Llywelyn was summoned five times to do homage; the first meeting had to be postponed because Edward was ill, but he did not attend on any subsequent occasion, even though on one of them Edward travelled to Chester to meet him. His excuse was that the king was sheltering Dafydd and Gruffydd.[50] Edward added to his grievances in 1275. At the time of his alliance with Simon de Montfort a marriage had been arranged with Simon's daughter Eleanor. The royal victory at Evesham and the subsequent exile of Simon's family in France put an end to these plans, but in 1275 the marriage was resurrected. After a ceremony by proxy in France Eleanor set out for Wales, but on the way her ship was captured and she was lodged in Windsor castle, to all intents and purposes a hostage. Llywelyn's principal causes for complaint were the asylum granted to the men who had planned to murder him and the detention of his wife; Edward's were the failure of the prince to do homage and to keep up the payments due for the Treaty of Montgomery, both of which he had freely undertaken to do in 1267. Llywelyn maintained that he would do homage and pay the arrears when the fugitives were handed over to him; Edward would consider doing this when Llywelyn had performed his obligations under the treaty. There was a final fruitless attempt to negotiate; indeed, the two sides never stopped talking. On 12 November 1276 Edward declared war.

The ensuing royal campaign was a model of its kind. Three armies moved into Wales, one from Chester, one from Montgomery and one from Carmarthen.[51] Llywelyn's territorial gains of the 1250s and 1260s were rapidly retaken and the other Welsh rulers flocked to make their peace. A royal fleet seized Anglesey and deprived Llywelyn of his main source of food as well as preventing him from moving out of Snowdonia. Work was begun on new castles at Flint, Rhuddlan, Ruthin, Builth and Aberystwyth to control the periphery of Gwynedd.[52] Llywelyn, having seen his principality melt away, had no choice but to submit and accept the terms set out on 9 November 1277 in the Treaty of Aberconwy.[53] These terms were severe. His territory was limited to that which he and Owain had held after the Treaty of Woodstock thirty years earlier. Owain was to be released from prison. He retained the title of prince of Wales, but only for his lifetime; the only homages which remained to him were those of five lords in what was left of his principality. A heavy fine was remitted at once but he undertook to pay all the money that he had agreed to pay at Montgomery. He also relinquished all claim to the Four Cantrefs and all his conquests outside Gwynedd. But, despite the severity of the treaty, he had not been destroyed; he was still a prince ruling in his hereditary lands, however much his state had been reduced.

Thus, ten years after Montgomery, the whole edifice of a Welsh principality had crumbled. It is easy to try and apportion blame; in reality the causes of Aberconwy are far more complex than foolhardiness and over-confidence on the part of Llywelyn or a determination to cut the prince down to size on the part of Edward. One of the fundamental problems was the Treaty of Montgomery itself. The principality of Wales had been recognised by the crown but it had no constitutional or administrative infrastructure and the creation of this would take time. The treaty had also confirmed Llywelyn's territorial gains; these had been at the expense of such magnates as the earl of Hereford and Roger Mortimer and they could not accept the permanence of such a settlement. It is easy to suggest with the advantage of hindsight that the prince might have been better advised to concentrate on extending his authority over those parts of Wales which were under native rule, but he could not have ignored the proffered allegiance of the Welsh of the march. Llywelyn also had difficulties with the church and by 1276 he was in dispute with the bishops of Bangor and St Asaph. These were great men in north Wales and the prince was seeking to impose his authority on them as he was on the other Welsh lords. Welsh rulers had traditionally enjoyed a good deal of authority over the church but attitudes had changed and the two bishops, Anian of Bangor and the prickly Anian II of St Asaph, turned to Edward for protection. Some historians have seen the revival of the de Montfort marriage as an error of judgement; such an alliance could reopen old wounds in England and Eleanor's brother had murdered his and Edward's cousin Henry of Almain in Italy.[54] But there was probably a good deal more to it than a desire to embarrass Edward. By this time Llywelyn must have been in his late forties and it does seem strange that he had not married and produced the heir who would guarantee the continuation of his principality; indeed, it even suggests a certain irresponsibility. The succession might, on the other hand, have been the price of Dafydd's support. If this were the case, it would explain why Llywelyn was so desperate to marry after the 1274 conspiracy and Dafydd's flight; he needed an heir quickly.

But the two great issues were homage and money. It is easy to argue that Llywelyn should have swallowed his pride and done homage to Edward, even though the latter had given asylum to the conspirators. But he had to consider his own political situation. His principality was a new institution and the firm government needed to hold it together had cut across many traditions and interests. His brother and heir and one of the greatest lords in Wales had conspired to murder him. He could not afford to let them escape; for the sake of his credibility they had to be brought back to face the consequences of their actions.

Nor could Edward afford to ignore Llywelyn's refusal of homage. He had not been long on the throne and in the previous decade the kingdom had endured a civil war. He could not allow any vassal, however eminent, to defy him and to withhold the homage and money due by treaty. Neither prince nor king, therefore, had any freedom of manoeuvre; neither could afford to compromise. The failure to continue paying the instalments due under the Treaty of Montgomery may reflect the financial pressures on Llywelyn. The principality of Wales was expensive. Castles had to be built, maintained and garrisoned. An army had to be kept in being, equipped and supplied. Service and loyalty had to be rewarded. And all this had to be paid for out of the limited resources of Gwynedd.[55] Llywelyn was in no position to tax the rest of Wales; the Powys and Deheubarth lords disposed of their own income and in the conquered lordships of the march he had to retain the goodwill of his new subjects. It has been suggested that his campaign in Glamorgan might, in the long term, have been aimed at securing the fertile lands of the Vale and that this might have solved his financial problems.[56] But the fact remains that he had his principality and Edward did not have his homage.

Relations were better after Aberconwy. Llywelyn did homage and in October 1278 he and Eleanor were married in Worcester cathedral; Edward paid for the festivities and gave away the bride (who was his cousin). The terms of the treaty were not as harsh as those of Woodstock had been and he was still prince of Wales. Recovery at some future date must have seemed possible and there is some evidence to suggest that he was taking steps to build up his position.[57] There is no simple explanation of the fact that five years after Aberconwy he would be dead in action against the king's armies, although some have accused Edward of bad faith and duplicity. There were disagreements after 1277 but they were not the kind which could only be resolved by war; most were over minor jurisdictional issues and Llywelyn's rights as prince. The most serious one with Gruffydd ap Gwenwynwyn over the cantref of Arwystli in the upper Severn valley, an area which had long been in dispute between

Gwynedd and Powys. The Treaty of Aberconwy had provided that territorial disputes in Wales should be settled by Welsh law and those in the march by the law of the march; earlier treaties had included similar provisions. But the problem about Arwystli was that Llywelyn claimed that it was in Wales, while Gruffydd argued that it was part of the march. After several inconclusive hearings the king, in 1280, appointed a commission to find out how actions involving Welsh princes and lords had been tried in the past; the evidence given to the commission includes a great deal of information about Welsh legal procedure in the thirteenth century.[58] On receiving its report in June 1281, Edward decided that English procedure should be used. This has often been seen as a deliberate snub to Llywelyn but the evidence did indicate that such procedure was being used in the prince's court. Llywelyn was disappointed but the Arwystli dispute was not in itself a *casus belli*; it had all the makings of a long-drawn-out legal battle but no more than that and it is likely that neither Edward nor Llywelyn wished to resort to arms, however much the latter may have been frustrated and irritated by delays and disputes.

The war, when it came in 1282, did not begin in Gwynedd or Arwystli. In the Four Cantrefs, two of which were ruled by Edward and two held by Llywelyn's brother Dafydd, tensions were running high, fuelled by insensitive royal officials who seem neither to have understood nor to have tried to appreciate the nuances of Welsh law and custom. Dafydd was in an ideal position to put himself at the head of an angry and resentful Welsh community and he may have been in touch with other lords elsewhere in Wales who were also feeling the heavy hand of royal administration. Llywelyn was still in touch with Edward and in February 1282 Eleanor, by now pregnant, wrote a friendly letter to her cousin in which she complained that more attention was being paid to her husband's opponents than to him.[59] The delays in dealing with his grievances were obviously getting on Llywelyn's nerves but there is nothing to suggest that he was preparing to go to war. It was Dafydd who took the final decisive step; on the night of 21 March 1282 he attacked Hawarden castle and the revolt spread through the Four

Cantrefs. A Welsh 'parliament' at Denbigh is said to have declared war.[60] The evidence certainly suggests preliminary planning; on the day after the attack on Hawarden the Welsh lords of northern Powys raided Oswestry and during the following week three important castles in the south-west were taken. In the previous war every Welsh lord outside Gwynedd had supported Edward; now all but two of them joined the war.

The outbreak took Edward by surprise; he felt that neither Llywelyn nor Dafydd had any cause for complaint. The pope was urging him to go on crusade, his help was being sought by the kings of France, Castile and Aragon and he was needed urgently in Gascony. His response was swift. Llywelyn and Dafydd were excommunicated and a campaign was planned to deal with them. Edward followed the strategy which had proved so effective in 1276–7, using armies based on Chester, Montgomery and Carmarthen to advance on Snowdonia.[61] Anglesey was again seized by a fleet from the Cinque Ports and the commander of the force there, Luke de Tany, was ordered to build a bridge of boats across the Menai Straits but not to cross it until the army from Chester, under the command of the king himself, had crossed the Conwy and entered Snowdonia. The aim was the unconditional surrender of Llywelyn and Dafydd. The king moved slowly and deliberately through the north-east to Rhuddlan, mopping up Welsh resistance on the way. The archbishop of Canterbury, John Pecham, made a bid to mediate; at the beginning of November he spent three days with Llywelyn and Dafydd at the former's court at Aber.[62] His visit achieved nothing; there was no meeting of minds and he obviously neither liked nor understood the Welsh. His register contains a number of documents, most of them from Welsh lords and communities outside Gwynedd, complaining of oppression by royal officials.[63] On his return he sent two sets of proposals to the prince, one calling for unconditional surrender and the other offering Llywelyn an earldom and a large estate in England in return for the surrender of Gwynedd and inviting Dafydd to go on an indefinite crusade.[64] Llywelyn was advised by his council to reject these terms and he did so in a dignified letter which has been compared with the Irish Remonstrance of 1317–18 and the Scottish Declaration of Arbroath of 1320 as an expression of burgeoning national consciousness.[65]

During the truce which had been agreed for the archbishop's visit Luke de Tany appears to have tried to establish a bridgehead on the mainland, but when his men were crossing the pontoon bridge it collapsed, the tide turned and the force was ambushed by the Welsh and cut to pieces on 6 November 1282. Llywelyn now took advantage of the victory which had been a blow to Edward's grand strategy and moved into mid-Wales with his army; on 11 December 1282 he was killed in circumstances which remain a mystery. His head was cut off, paraded before Edward's troops and displayed on the Tower of London and his body was buried in the Cistercian abbey of Cwm-hir. Eleanor had died in childbirth the previous June giving birth to a daughter, Gwenllian; she was sent by the king to the abbey of Sempringham in Lincolnshire where she ended her days as a nun in 1337. Dafydd carried on the fight in Snowdonia but the death of Llywelyn had taken the heart out of the Welsh. In June 1283 Dafydd was captured and the following October, after trial and sentence, he was executed with great barbarity at Shrewsbury. His head joined that of his brother on the Tower; his daughters followed their cousin to the cloister and his sons spent the rest of their lives in prison. The war ended on 9 July 1283 when each community in Gwynedd made its peace with the king.[66]

The war of 1282–3 marks the end of Welsh political independence. It poses many questions and the debate among historians goes on. The circumstances of Llywelyn's participation are far from clear. Edward assumed from the start that he was involved but there is no firm evidence of this until after Eleanor's death; this and the birth of a daughter may have led him to feel that he had nothing to lose, especially since it meant that Dafydd was now his undisputed heir.[67] By this time, too, he may have realised that he had to join in to control the situation and contain Dafydd's ambition. His death also raises questions. Had he broken out of Snowdonia and moved south to open a second front or had he been lured into a trap, possibly by the Mortimers? Was he in touch with disaffected elements in England? It was reported after his death that a treasonable letter had been found on his body. Why had he left the main body of his army when he met his death? Had he gone to meet local leaders to seek their support? Dafydd's role has also given rise to debate; the fact that he changed sides in 1263 and again in 1274 may suggest a lack of loyalty but it is also possible that these changes of allegiance were the result of the fundamental disagreement of an able man with policies which he saw as putting the principality and his inheritance in jeopardy. It is certainly simplistic to see Dafydd as Llywelyn's evil genius.

Was conquest inevitable? The end of Welsh independence was a combination of many causes. It has been said of the settlement of 1267 that it was founded 'not on a rock but on sand' and its terms contained the seeds of future trouble.[68] The position of the prince as an independent ruler who was also a vassal of the English crown raised constitutional questions in a century in which political relationships were becoming ever more clearly defined. Was the prince an independent ruler or a tenant-in-chief? During the Arwystli dispute Llywelyn argued that every province under the overlordship of the king of England had its own laws and customs, but this imperial argument, which foreshadowed the later clash between Edward and John Baliol in Scotland, was unacceptable to the king.[69] Reduced to the simplest terms, the Welsh and the Scots were willing to accept Edward as overlord as long as he did not interfere; Edward, however, saw his overlordship as involving something more and he insisted on the superiority of the prerogative and the dignity of the crown. In the Arwystli case, as in the matter of the Scottish succession in 1290, he was called in as an impartial umpire, but he regarded both issues as involving his prerogative. Some historians have seen a development of the intensification of the crown's lordship within the British Isles; the loss of Normandy and Anjou at the beginning of the century had led to a concentration on Britain and Ireland and Edward's efforts may have been intended to lead eventually to the creation of a united British kingdom under English rule.[70] Whether or not Edward had such a grand design remains an open question; it is also arguable that in Wales he responded to events (although Henry III had had a clear-cut policy in the 1240s, as witness the Anglo-Welsh treaties of that decade) and that his policy towards Scotland was conditioned by his experience in Wales.

The internal stresses and strains of Llywelyn's principality also played their part in its collapse. He was trying to create a single Welsh principality where no such institution had existed before and he had to create his own position and to be seen to be doing so. Unlike the Scottish king he was not part of the European royal network.[71] To hold his principality together he had to rule with a heavy hand; the way in which the other Welsh lords had made their peace with Edward in 1276–7 was, at least in part, a consequence of this but after the conquest it became clear that he had acted in the same way in his own hereditary lands in Gwynedd. A long list of grievances laid before the king's representatives in 1283 records the ways in which his own people were pushed to the limit to meet his constant need for money to pay for his principality and the extents made in Gwynedd after the conquest tell the same story.[72] His relationship with his own subjects was obviously under severe strain by 1282. This may be the context of an enigmatic entry in one text of *Brut y Tywysogyon* under 1282: 'and then there was effected the betrayal of Llywelyn in the belfry at Bangor by his own men'.[73] It is possible that some of the leaders of the community in Gwynedd had come to the conclusion that the price of Llywelyn's principality was too high. By 1282 the loyalty of some, at least, of the descendants of Ednyfed Fychan was questionable and one of his grandsons was among those killed at the abortive crossing of the Menai Straits.[74] Many may have taken advantage of the proclamation issued by Edward in 1282 which guaranteed the retention of their lands and privileges to those who submitted to him.[75] All these factors may have come together to bring about the events of 1282–3. It could be said that Llywelyn had to achieve too much too quickly and that the lack of any institutional infrastructure for the principality proved fatal. For the Welsh lords outside Gwynedd there was an alternative focus of loyalty in the shape of the crown; they had somewhere else to go. They cannot be stigmatised as quislings or traitors; their concern was to ensure the survival of their own lordships. Most of them did, in fact, join Llywelyn and Dafydd in 1282 but it may have been Gruffydd ap Gwenwynwyn of Powys who had the last laugh; he died in his bed of old age in 1286 and his marcher lordship, as it had become, was inherited by his son. In the end the conquest may have been the consequence of the ambiguity of the relationship created at Montgomery, the structural weaknesses of a new institution which had not had time to put down roots and the superior military, financial and political resources of the English crown.

4

SETTLEMENT AND CRISIS

The Edwardian Settlement

In the Statute of Wales, promulgated at Rhuddlan on 19 March 1284, Edward I set out his new arrangements for the government of the principality of north Wales.[1] The statute created three new counties in Gwynedd west of the Conwy: Anglesey, Caernarfon and Merioneth; a fourth county, Flint, was created in the north-east, but this was not part of the principality, being a Welsh extension of the earldom of Chester. In south-west Wales the counties of Carmarthen and Cardigan had been in existence since 1241.[2] In each county the crown was represented by a sheriff. At the head of the principality's administration was a new officer, the justiciar, a combination of governor, chief judge and military commander; the justiciar of north Wales or Snowdon was based at Caernarfon and that of south Wales at Carmarthen. In each principality the chief financial officer was the chamberlain, who presided over the Exchequer. A hierarchy of courts was established; the justiciar held his sessions in each county several times a year to deal with the pleas of the crown and the county court, presided over by the sheriff, met monthly. The commote became the hundred and the existing commote court became the hundred court, meeting every three weeks. The fourth court was the sheriff's tourn, another transplanted English institution, held in each commote at Easter and

Michaelmas; its principal function was the detection of crime. Perhaps the most successful of these institutions was the county court, which was more of an assembly of the county community than a judicial tribunal; here the king's wishes were explained and the community's grievances and concerns expressed. The Statute introduced English criminal law and procedure, although this was not so great a change in Gwynedd where criminal law had been developing along similar lines under the princes. Welsh civil law was, on the whole, retained. The changes in the southern counties were far less systematic, since much had happened there since 1241.

What these changes meant was that a new tier, in the shape of the county, was grafted on to the existing pattern of local administration. Under Edward I the justiciar was a trusted and experienced royal servant and the central administration was staffed by Englishmen. At the local level, however, the communities were still dominated by their traditional leaders who held the local offices; in the fourteenth century some leading Welshmen even held the office of sheriff. Edward I realised that Welshmen were best governed by Welshmen, a lesson which marcher lords had long since learned.[3] Typical of this class of native leaders was Sir Gruffydd ap Rhys or Sir Gruffydd Llwyd, a descendant of Ednyfed Fychan, who served at different times as sheriff of all the north Wales counties, who commanded troops from north Wales on several occasions and who was the leader of the royalist party in north Wales during the troubles of Edward II's reign; indeed, the descendants of Ednyfed or Wyrion Eden played a key part in the affairs of north Wales during the fourteenth century.[4] Another leading member of the same lineage was Sir Rhys ap Gruffydd, who dominated the principality of south Wales for some thirty years until his death in 1356.[5]

The administrative and legal changes contained in the Statute formed part of the Edwardian settlement of north Wales. This settlement also had military and economic aspects. To maintain order and minimise the risk of revolt Edward planned an elaborate system of castles. Some had already been built around the periphery of Gwynedd after 1276–7; now a further group was constructed within the principality itself and these castles are among the finest medieval military monuments in Europe.[6] Four of them, Caernarfon, Conwy and Harlech, begun immediately after the conquest, and Beaumaris, begun in the mid-1290s, were new, and two native castles, Cricieth in Caernarfonshire and Bere in Merioneth, were adapted and extended. The castles were the work of a single master mason, the Savoyard Master James of St George, whose work in his native province Edward may have seen when he was returning from the crusade at the beginning of his reign. Master James was one of the greatest masters of his craft; each of the castles was designed to fit the geographical features of the site. All of them except Bere could be relieved from the sea in the event of a siege. Their construction was a massive public works undertaking and it shows the logistic efficiency of Edward's government. A labour force was conscripted from all over England and supplies of stone, timber and other raw materials were carefully organised, as was money to pay the workers' wages. The diversion of the revenues of the vacant archbishoprics of York and Dublin helped to meet the colossal cost of the operation. Caernarfon took 38 years to complete and Beaumaris was never finished. It is difficult to say how effective the castles were. They were intended as a deterrent and it is fair to say that there was no revolt in north Wales for more than a century after their construction. Conwy, Harlech and Beaumaris were taken during the revolt of Owain Glyn Dŵr but otherwise they saw little action, apart from the Wars of the Roses, until the Civil War. Some were used from time to time for the custody of prisoners of war and state prisoners like the Lollards sent to Beaumaris in 1395 or Eleanor Cobham, duchess of Gloucester, who died in the same castle in 1452.[7] But they stand today as impressive military monuments; at Beaumaris and Harlech in particular the concentric castle reached its peak.

The castles were foreign bodies in the middle of the Welsh community. The economy of the principality could not easily be geared to victual them and this was one of the reasons for the establishment of plantation boroughs alongside them. These, colonised by English settlers, were intended as secure supply bases. Their charters followed a common form; the terms were made attractive to entice settlers who came from all parts of England. These burgesses enjoyed many commercial privileges but in the castle boroughs there was a measure of military control, the constable of the castle being *ex officio* mayor. At Caernarfon and Conwy the king paid for the construction of the town walls. As well as ensuring food supplies for the castles and their garrisons, the new boroughs were intended as centres for local trade; all buying and selling was to take place there and fines were imposed for trading elsewhere. Each borough had a weekly market and at least one fair during the year. Not all trade, however, was concentrated in the new foundations; those markets and fairs which had existed under the native princes at such places as Dolgellau and Bangor remained. Nor was every borough founded in association with a castle; when Beaumaris was established in 1296 the nearby Welsh urban community at Llan-faes was moved to a new site in south-east Anglesey and granted a charter of incorporation in 1303 as Newborough. Bala in Merioneth received its charter in 1324 and the two native Welsh towns in Llŷn, Nefyn and Pwllheli, were incorporated by the Black Prince in 1355.[8] Edward had already founded boroughs like Flint and Rhuddlan around the castles he had built after the war of 1276–7 and similar foundations emerged in the new marcher lordships of the north-east. All these fortified towns followed the pattern of the many *bastides* established in Gascony by successive English kings in the thirteenth century, a period which saw the foundation of new towns all over Europe.[9]

The settlement did not mean that Llywelyn's principality became part of the kingdom of England. Although the last native prince was dead, the principality recognised by the crown in 1267 was still a constitutional entity and Edward stepped into his predecessor's shoes. For most people there was little change; the leaders of the Welsh community on the whole supported and worked with the new règime. There was strong government but this was nothing new; if anything, Edward's rule may well have been less onerous than Llywelyn's had been and post-conquest sources reveal the extent of the last prince's harshness and rapacity. Between the conquest and the end of the century there were two revolts in Wales but these cannot in any way be seen as national protests aimed at reversing what had happened in 1282–3. The first, in Carmarthenshire in 1287, was led by Rhys ap Maredudd, a member of the Deheubarth dynasty. Rhys had been one of the two Welsh lords who had backed Edward in 1282 and he had expected a far more substantial reward than he had received. He had assumed that he would enjoy the traditional independence of a Welsh ruler, but the process of change had gone too far and he found himself subject to the constant interference of the royal authorities at Carmarthen. His revolt was easily put down by a massive show of force with extensive Welsh support; Rhys was unpopular and he may not have been forgiven for his failure to join the Welsh cause five years earlier. He was eventually captured and hanged at York.[10]

This was a personal protest by a disappointed man. The second revolt, in 1294–5, was far more serious, being a nation-wide rising with some indication of concerted planning.[11] It was led in the north by Madog ap Llywelyn, a member of a cadet branch of the Gwynedd dynasty whose father had been driven out of Meirionnydd by Llywelyn ap Gruffydd and who had tried without success to recover his patrimony in the courts. The leaders in the south-west were two members of the Deheubarth line, while in the south-east the movement was under the leadership of Morgan ap Maredudd of the former Gwent royal house. The revolt began with the advantage of surprise; the earl of Lincoln was defeated near Denbigh and the deputy-justiciar of south Wales was killed in an ambush. Llan-faes was burned, Caernarfon captured and the oppressive sheriff of Anglesey hanged. Edward had to abandon a projected campaign in France and set out for Wales in the winter; he spent Christmas 1294 under siege in Conwy castle. But superior royal resources turned the tide. The besieged castles were relieved from the sea, which proved the wisdom of their siting, and Madog himself was defeated at Maes Moydog in Powys. Order was eventually restored and Madog himself captured; he spent the rest of his life in the Tower of London, being still there in 1312, and one of his sons was still holding land in Anglesey in 1352.[12]

The revolt was put down by a massive display of military force; the cost of this unexpected campaign was so high that it contributed to major financial and constitutional crises in England in 1296 and 1297. But there were no reprisals; Edward seems to have realised why feelings in Wales were running so high in the 1290s. The aristocratic leaders of the 1294–5 revolt were really no more than figureheads; those behind it were the leaders of the native community, men like the descendants of Ednyfed Fychan in north Wales, and they were not concerned with the personal grievances of a handful of dispossessed lords. The real grievances were those of the community; these included excessive financial demands, based on the abnormal circumstances of Llywelyn's last years, insensitive officials, the levying of troops in Wales for service in France and the demand for a subsidy from Wales in 1291–2. Although the revolt disrupted Edward's plans and cost him a great deal of money, he does seem to have realised that it had been caused by real problems and there was a conscious attempt to remedy Welsh grievances.[13] The leaders of the community had spoken and the king listened. Madog ap Llywelyn was not executed, while within a few years of the revolt Morgan ap Maredudd had been knighted and was leading troops to the king's wars.

Edward could not legislate for Wales as a whole; the march remained and to pay some of the political and military debts incurred by the 1282 war he had to create four new marcher lordships in north-east Wales. Nevertheless, he did seize every opportunity to extend his authority over individual lords and lordships, as in 1291 when the earl of Gloucester, lord of Glamorgan, invaded the earl of Hereford's lordship of Brecon and took plunder.[14] Both lords were punished by the king, not for making war (which was their right as marcher lords) but for disobeying a royal command to cease fighting. The subsidy of 1291–2 was levied in the march as well as in the royal lands and Edward intervened there on several other occasions. He was a strong and masterful ruler who could act in this way with impunity; his successors, however, were unable to follow his example and a consistent royal policy towards the lords was out of the question as more and more lordships passed by marriage or inheritance into the possession of English magnates.

Wales and Fourteenth-Century Politics

In 1301 Edward's eldest surviving son, Edward of Caernarfon, became prince of Wales; the principality would in future be conferred on the heir to the throne, although there were periods when there was no prince. When Edward I died in 1307 the prince became king as Edward II. After his father's strong rule there was bound to be a reaction and the new king did not have the experience or the character to contain it. He was faced with a powerful baronial party, many of whose leaders had power-bases in the march. In Wales, too, there were problems; the death of the last native lord of Powys in 1309 led to a long struggle for power there and in 1314 the young earl of Gloucester was killed at Bannockburn, leaving no heir. The misgovernment of the lordship by its keeper led in 1315–16 to a revolt led by Llywelyn Bren, a descendant of the Welsh lords of Senghennydd; a great deal of damage was done but Llywelyn surrendered in 1316.[15] The king's troubles in Scotland also had Welsh repercussions; after Bannockburn a Scottish fleet was active in the Irish Sea and there was a fear that the Scots would link up with disaffected elements in Wales, especially following the Bruce brothers' invasion of Ireland in 1315. There is evidence to suggest that some of the leaders of the native community in north Wales were making contact with the Scots and concessions made to the communities of the northern and southern principalities at the parliament held at Lincoln in 1315 may reflect the concern of the authorities.[16] Garrisons were reinforced from time to time and there was to be a Scottish raid on Beaumaris as late as 1381.

During the reign of Edward II Wales played its most prominent part in fourteenth-century English politics. Marcher lords like the earl of Pembroke and Roger Mortimer of Chirk were important figures in England and the leader of the baronial opposition to Edward II, the king's cousin Thomas, earl of Lancaster, was himself a marcher lord, having inherited the lordship of Denbigh from his father-in-law, the earl of Lincoln; it was in the march that the crisis which was to lead to civil war erupted.[17] This was the result of the division of the Gloucester inheritance in Glamorgan; following the death of the earl of Gloucester at Bannockburn, his widow had feigned pregnancy for two years but the inheritance was eventually divided between his three sisters and their husbands. One of these husbands was the king's favourite, the younger Hugh Despenser; he was greedy and Glamorgan itself, the largest marcher lordship, fell to his share. As he had already received extensive lands in south Wales from the king, this made him the greatest power there and a threat to the delicate balance of marcher power. The result, in 1321, was war in the march and the exile of Despenser and his father; Edward then turned on his opponents and in 1322 Lancaster was defeated at Boroughbridge and executed. In 1326, in the final crisis of his reign, Edward II fled to Wales and was captured near Neath; his wife's lover, Roger Mortimer of Wigmore, who was instrumental in his downfall, was also a marcher magnate. The Welsh of the principality supported the king in all the troubles of his reign; men tended, of course, to follow their own lords and he had been theirs since 1301, and the Mortimer family was probably much disliked. But there may also have been some personal loyalty, perhaps because he had been born in Wales. It is possible that the murder of Edward at Berkeley in 1327 was the result of a plot hatched in north Wales to rescue him, news of which had reached Mortimer; some of the leaders of the north Wales community were subsequently imprisoned for a time.[18]

With the deposition and death of Edward II the political honeymoon of the leaders of the Welsh community and the English crown came to an end. Edward I and Edward II had depended on them to govern at the local level and they had held most of the offices. But now there was a change, especially after

Edward III's assumption of personal power in 1330. The new king seems not to have trusted the Welsh and he saw his lands in Wales primarily as a source of men and money for his wars. Offices in the principality were used to pay his creditors; the most blatant example was the virtual alienation of the county of Merioneth to Sir Walter de Mauny in 1341.[19] The creation of the king's eldest son Edward, better known as the Black Prince, as prince of Wales in 1343 ushered in a period of more active and positive government in the principality, the object being to extract as much revenue as possible. The new government was so active that it even tried to extend its authority over the march; some marcher lords protested and the consequence was a statute of 1354 which stated that they held directly of the king.[20] Within the northern principality the activities of the new regime seem to have led to fear and resentment on the part of the community's leaders, culminating in 1345 in the assassination of the prince's attorney in north Wales by a band led by the head of the senior line of the descendants of Ednyfed Fychan.[21] There were similar pressures in the earldom of Chester; the system of farming offices led to the office-holders seeking to make the maximum profit and in Flintshire it exacerbated a long-established culture of extortion and misgovernment in which Welsh officials impartially oppressed both Welsh and English tenants.[22]

It was the military needs of Edward III and his son which turned the screw. Wales, both principality and march, had supplied soldiers for the royal armies ever since the conquest and some leading Welshmen had a long record of military experience. Troops were summoned from each county and lordship by commission of array; most of them were infantrymen armed with bows and spears. Seven thousand men were raised from Wales for the Crécy campaign in 1346 and in the same year some Welsh units were issued with a green and white uniform, probably in the interests of maintaining discipline among one of the most unruly sections of the English army.[23] Welshmen also served in the Poitiers campaign of 1355–6 and with the Black Prince in Castile in 1367. There is no evidence of any great profit coming to Wales from the spoils of war but some, like Sir Hywel ap Gruffydd from Caernarfonshire and Sir Gregory Sais from Flintshire, did make a name for themselves. Sir Hywel did such good service at Poitiers with his battleaxe that he came to be known as Sir Hywel of the Axe and it was later claimed that the Black Prince had had the axe put in a place of honour in his hall and served with a daily ration of food.[24] The French wars did have some direct impact on Wales from time to time; there were fears of raids by French and Castilian ships and in the 1340s concern was expressed in north Wales about the levying of troops for service abroad because of this.[25]

The Medieval Society and Economy

As in the rest of Europe, the fundamental division in medieval Welsh society was that between free and unfree. For the free the main social bond was kinship; it was through his descent that the free man knew exactly who he was, and his place in society, his status and his title to land depended on his membership of a kindred or lineage group. Free land was hereditary land and each individual member of the group was entitled to a share, but there was no right of alienation; the interest of an individual has been described as 'a bundle of rights and inheritance'.[26] The land-holding group was called the *gwely* (bed or resting-place) in some parts of Wales and the *gafael* (holding) in others. The size of these holdings varied, as did the number of members and, therefore, the shares of individuals. However, this pattern was already beginning to break up in the first half of the fourteenth century. Some enterprising free tenants were beginning to acquire land in their own right; they could not buy but it was possible to use a kind of gage, the conveyance in *tir prid*, which involved the pledging of land in return for a sum of money.[27] The pledge was never redeemed and thus the transaction amounted to a permanent conveyance. This device seems to have originated before the conquest and hundreds of *tir prid* deeds survive from the end of the thirteenth century onwards. The beginning of a process of estate-building may be seen in the fourteenth century;

substantial sums of money were spent on land by such men as Tudur ab Ithel Fychan, the founder of the Mostyn estate, in Flintshire and Gwilym ap Gruffydd ap Tudur (d. 1376) in Anglesey and Caernarfonshire.[28] These men did not limit their activities to acquiring land under Welsh law; they also took advantage of the means provided by English land law, sometimes by licence, but more often than not without, and more land actually changed hands in this way than it did by *tir prid*.

The wealth of free tenants varied enormously. Many were very poor, living close to the margin; this was essentially a society of peasant proprietors, most holdings being of ten acres or less, although they usually included grazing rights as well. For a large part of the population a bad harvest, a fine or the marriage of a daughter could spell disaster. But at the upper levels of society there could be substantial wealth. Iorwerth ap Llywarch of the lordship of Denbigh, the chamberlain of Earl Thomas of Lancaster, had 1,200 acres and when Cynwrig Sais of Northop in Flintshire died in 1311 he had £120 in ready cash as well as a good deal of land and personal property.[29] Llywelyn Bren, the leader of the 1315 revolt in Glamorgan, had 77 oxen, 552 head of cattle and 191 sheep, and his personal property included eight books, three of them being Welsh ones.[30] These were the men who dominated and ruled their communities, holding their offices under the crown or marcher lords; they formed the Welsh political nation. They had also taken the place of the princes as patrons of the poets. The fourteenth century saw the emergence of a new and simpler kind of poetic diction which took the place of the complex ceremonial poetry of the court poets whose *raison d'être* had ended with the conquest; the outstanding poet of the fourteenth century, Dafydd ap Gwilym, may with justice be described as one of the leading poets of medieval Europe, while Iolo Goch gave voice to the political aspirations of his patrons.[31] The poets, who served a rigorous apprenticeship to their craft, came from the ranks of the leaders of the community or the *uchelwyr*, a word not easily translated but perhaps best rendered in English as 'squirearchy'; some held local offices themselves and they certainly did not live in a kind

93

of Celtic bardic twilight. Nor was the literary tradition, nourished by the *uchelwyr*, restricted to poetry; many prose texts, both secular and religious, survive, often being translations of French or Latin originals, and these can shed light on the interests of the patrons who commissioned them.[32] The leaders of Welsh society were well aware of the world outside Wales; at the end of the fourteenth century, for example, a popular work of travel, *The Journey of Brother Odoricus*, was translated for a squire in the Tawe valley near Swansea, which shows that there were those in Wales who had heard of China and Tibet.[33]

The unfree had once been in the majority but their number was declining in the fourteenth century, although they were still responsible for half the land revenue of north Wales at its end. The bondman or *taeog* was born to his status but could be manumitted, usually on payment of a fine. He could be bought, sold or bequeathed but this was usually a matter of conveying the right to his services and the land on which he had his holding; it may be described as the sale or bequest of lordship rather than a traffic in human flesh. Like his fellows elsewhere, he was subject to various restrictions; he could not marry, live elsewhere, take holy orders or make a will without the consent of his lord and this had to be paid for. By the fourteenth century these restrictions were coming to be regarded as nothing more than a means for the prince or the lord to raise revenue.[34] He had formerly owed food renders and labour services but these had almost invariably been commuted. Bond communities were usually separate from free ones and tended to be smaller. The most onerous form of bond tenure was one under which dues and rents were assessed on the community as a whole, rather than on individuals, so that the individual burden depended on the number of adult males; this tenure was called *tir cyfrif* (reckoned land) but many bondmen were held by *tir gwelyog*, which was more akin to free tenure.[35] The economic position of bondmen could vary as much as that of free tenants; despite the disabilities which went with unfree status, some accumulated substantial amounts of land and moveable wealth. Some services were also owed by free tenants and these, with those of the bondmen, are set out in several detailed surveys like those of St David's (1326), Denbigh (1334), Anglesey and Caernarfonshire (1352) and Bromfield and Yale (1391).[36]

English communities were not restricted to the boroughs and to the Englishries of lowland marcher lordships. In some lordships, especially those near the English border, there might be many English settlers, but in others they were few and far between. In the lordship of Denbigh at least 10,000 acres were in English hands by 1334 and as much of this settlement had been facilitated by the removal of Welsh tenants to less desirable land, relations were not always easy. Some English communities were long-established but others, especially in the new marcher lordships of the north-east, were of more recent origin and it was here that tensions were most common. The division between Welsh and English was one of the basic lines of demarcation, but it was not always clearly defined and officials were frequently faced with complicated questions of status which might turn on land tenure or inheritance rather than on ethnic origin.[37] Status was a matter of such things as law and inheritance customs and the two peoples often lived under different laws in a state of mutual hostility, suspicion and incomprehension. However, intermarriage was common; within a generation or two English families might become Welsh and such names as Puleston, Hanmer, Havard and Stradling bear witness to this.

The position of women in medieval Welsh society could vary a great deal.[38] In the north-east they could not inherit land but in the principality they could do so under the terms of the Statute of Wales. Marriage was seen as a civil contract rather than as a sacrament and, like any other contract, it could be terminated; Welsh law had always made provision for this. At the upper levels of society marriages were generally arranged and many were within the same lineage group. Under Welsh law the right of a son to a share in the inheritance depended on recognition by his father rather than on being born in wedlock.[39] There is certainly evidence of women participating in economic life and, in the principality, of their holding land in their own right; in Merioneth in 1292–3 about 10 per cent of the taxpayers were women and this is not the only evidence.[40] Surviving judicial records show that in a violent society women could be every bit as violent as their menfolk and they also show that they were not averse to crime.

Medieval Welsh towns have tended to be associated with English settlement, but Welsh men and women were very ready to live in them and there was a pre-conquest urban tradition. Many marcher foundations, like Tenby, Pembroke and Cardiff, were entirely English, but there were others with a strong Welsh element in their population and these were not only such native centres as Llanrwst, Nefyn and Pwllheli; there was a considerable Welsh presence in, for example, Ruthin, Oswestry, Monmouth and Brecon and by the second half of the century the Welsh had found their way into Carmarthen, the administrative centre of the southern principality.[41] There are also cases in the fourteenth century of Welsh burgesses being expelled from some of the northern castle boroughs which were, after all, intended as English colonies.[42] Some prosperous English burgesses were to buy land in the hinterland of their towns or to marry Welsh heiresses and they, too, joined the ranks of the *uchelwyr*. There were no large towns in Wales and no urban patriciates, although most were dominated by a small group of families. But some towns were more important and more prosperous than others, although their importance lay in their role as service and trading centres or ports, rather than in any industrial activity. The leading towns in medieval Wales were probably Cardiff, Swansea, Brecon, Carmarthen and Haverfordwest in the south and Beaumaris, Caernarfon, Conwy, Denbigh and Wrexham in the north.

The medieval Welsh economy was based on agriculture. The pattern was one of mixed farming, with some crops being grown even on the poorest soils. Much cultivation was carried on in open fields, although in upland areas the infield–outfield pattern was probably common. Ploughing and harrowing had been among the labour services due from bondmen. Wheat, barley, oats, rye, beans and peas were grown; the scarcity of good-quality arable land in most parts of the country meant that oats were the predominant crop and wheat was often grown for the market rather than for consumption. There is some evidence of the rotation of crops, especially in those marcher lordships where there was still direct seigneurial exploitation in the first half of the century.[43] Crop yields in the more fertile south-east seem to have been much the same as contemporary yields in England but elsewhere they were considerably less. Many tenants, free as well as bond, owed suit of mill to the prince or the lord, but contemporary surveys show that many lineage groups had their own mills. Most of these were powered by water, but a few windmills did exist; one was built at Newborough in Anglesey in 1305 and there were three at Tenby in 1330.[44]

But cattle were the mainstay of the rural economy; already many were being exported to English markets and marcher lords used their Welsh lands to supply their households. In 1349 more than 400 head of cattle were driven from Brecon to Essex for the Bohun family.[45] Many cattle and pigs were slaughtered and salted down at the beginning of the winter but most surplus animals were sold. Large-scale sheep-farming, the activity particularly associated with Wales today, did not really gather momentum until the fourteenth century, if not later, in many upland areas. The real pioneers of sheep-farming had been the Cistercians and this was the result of massive grants to them of upland pastures by twelfth-century rulers. At the end of the thirteenth century Margam had over 5,000 sheep and Neath nearly 5,000; Tintern had 3,264.[46] The best Welsh wool was that produced by Tintern, which was comparable with the product of the great Yorkshire abbeys. That from Basingwerk abbey on Deeside was also of high quality, but most wool from Wales went to produce a cheaper cloth. By the fourteenth century some marcher lords were going over to sheep-farming and over 3,000 fleeces were exported from the lordship of Brecon in 1370; the Greys, lords of Dyffryn Clwyd, had a flock of between 2,000 and 3,000 sheep and the earl of Arundel had over 3,000 at Clun in 1372.[47] During the century there was an increasing emphasis on the production of cloth rather than on the export of raw wool; in the north-east in particular the manufacture of cloth was coming to play an increasing part in the economy and lords were investing in the construction of fulling-mills.[48]

A significant contribution to the rural economy was made by the forest and its resources were carefully and efficiently managed.[49] The forest yielded building timber, firewood, charcoal, bark for tanning, ashes for dyeing, pannage for pigs and honey, the usual sweetening agent, from wild bees; other products included peat, rushes and bracken for litter and it was a centre for such industrial activities as the making of wooden utensils. There was an important herring fishery in the Irish Sea, based on such ports as Nefyn, Pwllheli and Aberystwyth and seals were hunted on the offshore islands; the rivers also yielded fish, which was a valuable part of the diet and both lords and free tenants might build weirs and fish-traps. The mineral wealth of Wales was being exploited, especially by the Cistercians; both Margam and Neath were mining coal from the middle of the thirteenth century.[50] Coal was also mined in Pembrokeshire and in the north-east and the death of a man called Bleddyn in a coal mine on Deeside in 1346 may be one of the first recorded fatalities in that industry.[51] Lead was mined by the Cistercians of Basingwerk and Strata Florida and the lead-miners at Holywell and at Minera near Wrexham lived and worked in self-contained communities under their own laws and customs; there was also some iron- and copper-mining.[52] The production of wool and the mining of coal and minerals were not the only economic activities carried on by the Cistercians; several abbeys bred horses and some owned ships and traded. Some, too, like Tintern and Margam, enjoyed the income from urban property in Cardiff and Bristol. A Cistercian abbot had to be a shrewd business man as well as a spiritual father to his monks.

The main exports of Wales were wool, dairy products, hides and timber; some slate was already being exported from Caernarfonshire and Anglesey millstones had a high reputation. The most valuable import was wine and the leading ports, among them Chepstow, Carmarthen, Tenby, Haverfordwest and Beaumaris, had their own ships and an extensive foreign trade. Wool was exported from Carmarthen in 1354 in ships from Bristol, Tenby, Waterford and Spain and the town was visited by merchants from Germany, Bruges, Venice and Lombardy. In 1392–3 ships brought wine to the port of Milford from Gascony, Nantes, La Rochelle and Spain; the evidence of contemporary poetry bears witness to the presence of many exotic delicacies on the tables of the poets' patrons, showing that Wales was certainly a part of the extensive and sophisticated network of medieval trade.[53] The markets of the leading border towns, such as Chester, Shrewsbury and Leominster, played an important part in the Welsh economy and at the end of the thirteenth century merchants from Chester and Bristol had been influential figures in north and south Wales; the interests of the Chester merchant William of Doncaster had extended as far as Anglesey.[54] There is not enough surviving evidence to draw any hard and fast conclusions about wages and prices in late medieval Wales, but what information is available suggests that levels were much the same as in England; the same scarcity of evidence makes it dangerous to speculate about the wealth of Wales, although one historian has suggested that at the end of the thirteenth century Anglesey was richer than some parts of England, including Bedfordshire and the West Riding of Yorkshire.[55] But the evidence and the statistical base for valid comparisons are not really there, nor is it possible to offer any estimate of the population; all that can be said is that the population of Wales was certainly declining during the fourteenth century.

Crisis, Plague and Slump

For Wales, as for most of Europe, the fourteenth century may be described as a period of crisis. By the end of the thirteenth century, if not before, the steadily increasing population had outstripped the amount of land which could be brought into cultivation. This was accompanied by a deterioration in the climate; colder and wetter weather now meant poorer harvests and a greater risk of famine. This came between 1315 and 1317, when the harvest failed over much of western Europe for three years in succession. Such a catastrophe did not only affect the immediate food supply; it also imperilled the seed-corn which was needed for the following year. Although there is little direct evidence for the impact of this disaster on Wales, there is enough to indicate that the country was affected. There was some recovery after 1317 but bad harvests were not uncommon and in the 1320s there came a series of livestock epidemics against a background of a steady decline in agricultural prices, which in turn affected tax yields. All this was accompanied by natural disasters which may have been a consequence of climatic change; a large part of the lands of the town of Newborough disappeared under sand-dunes following a violent storm in 1330 and the entire town of Kenfig in Glamorgan was gradually to suffer the same fate.[56]

All these problems, however, were overshadowed in the middle of the century by the bubonic plague pandemic usually known as the Black Death. This began in Central Asia and made its way along trade routes into Europe, reaching Britain at Melcombe Regis near Weymouth in 1348. From here it spread rapidly, the fleas which carried it travelling with merchandise. It seems to have come into Wales by way of the south-east and by March 1349 it had reached the lordship of Abergavenny in Gwent, the lord's son being among its victims.[57] It then moved north along the border through the lordships of Whittington and Chirk, leaving a trail of mortality behind it. Flintshire was hit very hard and by June 1349 it had reached Ruthin; in the lordship of Dyffryn Clwyd 139 died in a fortnight and it did not reach its peak there until late August. The plague had reached Carmarthen, probably having come by sea, at the end of March 1349; it swept through the counties of Carmarthen and Cardigan during the summer and many tenants fled, often, probably, in vain.[58] It is impossible, on the basis of the surviving evidence, to examine its effect on every part of Wales; there is no information, for example, about its impact on the county of Merioneth and very little for Powys. However, the north does seem to have suffered more than the south. Anglesey and Caernarfonshire were badly affected and at Degannwy in the latter county almost all the bondmen succumbed; according to the English chronicler Geoffrey le Baker one-third of the population of Wales was wiped out and the Anglesey poet Gruffydd ap Maredudd ap Dafydd begged God to show mercy to Gwynedd.[59] In the Caernarfonshire commote of Nantconwy there were 149 bond tenants before the plague but only 47 afterwards. There were further visitations in 1361–2 and 1369 and these wrought particular havoc in those parts of south and south-east Wales which had escaped the worst effects in 1349; there were also many local outbreaks and when the bishop of St Asaph made his will in 1373 he referred to 'the plague which violently rages in these days'.[60] The effects of all these attacks can be seen in surviving records for several years.

The results of the plague were far-reaching. There was an immediate drop in revenue in both the principality and the march because the rate of mortality was higher among bondmen who carried a heavier burden of dues and rents and who were more likely to live in nucleated communities. Before the plague land had been at a premium and the authorities had had no difficulty in finding tenants for escheat lands; now, with the death of so many tenants, there was a glut of untenanted land and much arable land had to be let for grazing. Enterprising survivors were able to snap up vacant tenements and this contributed significantly to the growth of new estates. The breakdown of the traditional kindred-based system of free tenure was accelerated, as was the development of a market in land. Small men were selling out to wealthier neighbours and the consequence was the emergence of a class of landless men whose problems were aggravated by the fact that the direct exploitation of demesne land by marcher lords no longer paid. Demesne farming had been abandoned in some lordships before the plague; now many more lords rented out their demesnes, in effect creating family farms which had no need for extra labour. This was the only way in which lords could maintain their revenue; lordship, at least in economic terms, came to mean little more than a mechanism for the collection of rent and this transformed the relationship of lord and tenant. Much land was turned over permanently to pasture and the development of sheep-farming, particularly in the marcher lordships of mid-Wales, gathered momentum.

Another consequence of the plague was migration; in the years after 1349 there was a large increase in the number of avowry tenants moving into marcher lordships and the principality from elsewhere. There had always been a good deal of migrant labour in Wales, especially at harvest time, but avowry, the process whereby immigrants placed themselves under the protection of the prince or the lord, involved permanent settlement.[61] This was a common phenomenon all over Europe in the period following the pestilence; land and work were available and there were opportunities for many to better themselves. Many of those who moved were bondmen, but the authorities, only too glad to find tenants for vacant land, were not disposed to ask too many questions. In the immediate aftermath of the plague there was also a considerable effect on the labour market. Labour was scarce and the survivors were able to demand higher wages which employers were willing to pay. The fact that most labour services in Wales had already been commuted meant that there was more emphasis on wage labour. The authorities were, however, quick to react; the 1351 Statute of Labourers seems to have been enforced in Wales and agreements were made between individual marcher lordships for the return of fugitive bondmen.[62]

There was some temporary recovery after the plague but the long-term trend was downwards. The loss of revenue in some lordships was to be permanent; in Ogmore it fell by at least 30 per cent.[63] Tenements were amalgamated and cottages fell into ruin. The rural depopulation which followed the plague was to continue through the fifteenth century; accounts show whole townships let for grazing.[64] Many mills are recorded as being in decay; less land under the plough meant less corn and a substantial surplus of milling capacity. It is possible that many deserted village sites await excavation; the absence of old-established nucleated village sites over much of Wales may owe as much to the plague and to the consequent depopulation as to traditional patterns of settlement. The second half of the fourteenth century seems generally to have been a period of slump and there are few signs of recovery; some contemporary accounts also hint at more poverty, although it has to be added that a good deal more investigation is needed. The effect on Welsh towns is not easy to assess; some, like Wrexham, are known to have been prosperous but the castle boroughs of the northern principality certainly had problems in the last decade of the century and in Pembroke in the 1390s no fewer than 25½ burgages were vacant.[65] The fourteenth century has generally been seen as a period of crisis and recession and it is easy to lay all the blame for this on the plague; this certainly made a bad situation worse, but climatic change, famine, livestock epidemics and the pressure on arable land arising from over-population all played their part. Indeed, one historian has suggested that the impact of the plague on Europe generally was 'more purgative than toxic' and that it brought the population down to a sustainable level.[66] The century undoubtedly saw the beginning of the transition to a new social and economic pattern based on the landed estate on the one hand and on wage labour on the other. The trend had already begun before the plague but now the process was accelerated.

The problems of fourteenth-century Wales were not only social and economic. This was a period of political tension, highlighted by one episode in particular in the second half of the century, when the last heir of the Gwynedd dynasty made a bid to recover his patrimony. Owain ap Thomas ap Rhodri, also known as Owain Lawgoch (Red Hand), was the great-nephew of Llywelyn ap Gruffydd.[67] His grandfather, Llywelyn's youngest brother, had sold his rights in Gwynedd and had retired to England as a royal pensioner. Owain's father Thomas had inherited lands in Cheshire, Surrey and Gloucestershire, along with a small Welsh lordship on the Shropshire–Powys border. Owain himself seems to have spent his youth abroad; he returned after his father's death in 1363 to claim his inheritance,

but in 1369 his lands were confiscated because he had gone over
to the French, in whose service he commanded a free company of
Welshmen. The French knew him as Yvain de Galles and were
well-aware of who he was and of his claim to the principality;
Charles V and his advisers saw the potential of an invasion of
Wales and of a revolt there on Owain's behalf after the renewal
of Anglo-French hostilities in 1369 and they were willing to back
him. At the end of 1369 an expedition under Owain's command
set out from Harfleur but was driven back by storms. A further
attempt was made in 1372; in a proclamation Owain set out his
claim and once again a fleet sailed from Harfleur. On the way it
attacked Guernsey but went no further; Owain was diverted to
Castile to persuade its king to join the French in an attack on La
Rochelle, then held by the English. The mission was successful;
an English fleet was annihilated by the Castilians and the town
surrendered. But there were no more attempts to win back
Owain's principality, although he may have made an abortive
bid for Castilian aid. From 1372 Owain and his company were
active in French service and in 1375 they were defeated by the
citizens of Berne in the battle of Fraubrunnen, having been
employed by one of the leading French commanders, Enguerrand
de Coucy, in an unsuccessful attempt to overthrow the duke of
Austria; the Swiss took great pride in having defeated him. For
the next three years he was campaigning against the English in
south-west France and in the summer of 1378 he was besieging
the fortress of Mortagne-sur-Gironde which controlled the
maritime approach to Bordeaux, the centre of English power in
Guienne. It was during this siege that he was assassinated by an
English agent, John Lambe, who had inveigled himself into his
service and who was paid £20 for killing him.

This was the end of the direct male line of the Gwynedd
dynasty. It is easy to dismiss Owain ap Thomas ap Rhodri as 'a
pawn in the Anglo-French struggle' and as one of a long line of
ineffective exiled pretenders; he was certainly not the last one
from Britain to seek French aid.[68] Nor was his cause, however
advantageous it may have been to France, one of Charles V's
priorities. Nevertheless, the French were prepared to invest

considerable sums in him and this suggests that they expected a response in Wales. The surviving Welsh evidence certainly suggests some alarm on the part of the authorities; castles were reinforced and defensive arrangements were made more than once and in Flintshire a former sheriff of the county and a descendant of Ednyfed Fychan to boot was twice accused of communicating with Owain, of sending him money and of receiving letters from him. Two of his sons were also with Owain in France, one of them being his lieutenant and the inheritor of his company after his death. It is ironic that this same sheriff had been the subject in 1358 and 1359 of petitions against his oppressive and extortionate rule and that money raised in the name of the Black Prince may have found its way to Owain. Had judicial records from other parts of Wales survived, we might well know more about the extent of Welsh support for the last heir of Gwynedd and particularly about the role of the descendants of Ednyfed Fychan.

Owain was certainly considered enough of a threat to be eliminated. There were Welshmen in French service; the names of 38 of them were presented by a Flintshire jury in 1374 and some of these names also appear in the musters of Owain's company in France. There was no lack of foreign mercenaries in the French armies; indeed, the employment of foreigners has always been part of the French military tradition. Some of these men were probably deserters or adventurers, but there was more than one reason for disaffection in late fourteenth-century Wales. Residual anti-English sentiment may have been fuelled by the disillusion of the leaders of the native community after the fall of Edward II in 1327 as well as by the social and economic problems of the time. A general climate of restlessness and discontent all over Europe followed the plague; it was a period of disorientation and popular revolts. Many messianic and millenarian movements emerged; these were usually social and religious but in Wales they seem to have acquired a political dimension. It is possible that, although the Welsh political nation had accepted the new Edwardian order in 1284, there may have been an undercurrent of nostalgia. The presence of the heir of Gwynedd in France after 1369 could well have acted as a catalyst. The restoration of the native dynasty may have come to be seen as a matter of practical politics, especially in the context of contemporary tensions. There had in Wales been a long tradition of prophetic poetry, calling on a leader, often addressed as Owain, to return to his people; after 1282 this poetry, often very obscure and allusive, had a new lease of life and some of it is almost certainly addressed to Owain ap Thomas ap Rhodri.[69] There is no evidence that he ever visited Wales or that he could even speak Welsh, but the poets and their patrons knew very well who he was and what he represented. There was an alternative to the house of Plantagenet, which may itself have been a scapegoat for all the current troubles; those who hailed Owain and who worked for his return were hard-headed men of affairs, not romantic visionaries. After his death he became a Sleeping Hero, asleep in a cave waiting for the call; given the circumstances of his death, far away from Wales, and given the fact that few in Wales had ever seen him, alive or dead, this was hardly surprising. People have always found it hard to accept the death of a charismatic leader and folk-tales about Owain Lawgoch, asleep in a cave, survived into the twentieth century.[70]

Nor was Owain the only problem facing the authorities. The last quarter of the fourteenth century saw a steady decline in standards of public order. Economic difficulties and the demands of tax-collectors played their part in this and the presence of many former soldiers who could not readjust and settle down to civilian life after years of service in France did not help. Every squire had his *plaid* or retinue of kinsmen and dependants, many recruited from old soldiers. In 1391 one Flintshire squire led what amounted to a private army against his cousin and in 1385 the deputy-justiciar of south Wales was murdered on the road between Cardigan and Carmarthen by a local *uchelwr*; in Cardiganshire there were complaints of misgovernment and corruption.[71] There was discontent, too, among the clergy. Most leading Welsh churchmen were drawn from the ranks of the *uchelwyr* and in the first half of the century they had not lacked preferment, but after about 1350 the Welsh church came to be seen as a source of patronage and there was increasing royal and papal interference in senior appointments.[72] Well-qualified and educated Welshmen were ignored in favour of royal clerks, chaplains and confessors and the result was a rising tide of clerical resentment. The parish clergy, whose fixed incomes were hit by inflation and who were often as poor as most of their parishioners, were also increasingly disaffected. With all these tensions at every level of society, Wales in the last decade of the fourteenth century was ready for an explosion and that explosion came in 1400.

5

Rebellion and Revenge

Owain Glyn Dŵr

On 16 September 1400, at Glyndyfrdwy in Merioneth, Owain ap Gruffydd Fychan or Owain Glyn Dŵr, lord of Glyndyfrdwy and Cynllaith Owain, was proclaimed prince of Wales and thus began a revolt which was to last for some ten years and which stands at the centre of the history of late medieval Wales. Owain himself was a descendant of the dynasty of northern Powys and was one of the surviving handful of native Welsh lords of royal descent who had retained a small portion of what was left of their patrimony. His ancestors appear from time to time in the records; they seem to have had close relations with their powerful neighbour the earl of Arundel, lord of Chirk and Oswestry and later of Bromfield and Yale, and his father had been steward of the lordship of Oswestry and keeper of the lordship of Ellesmere.[1] His grandmother had been a member of a leading marcher family, the Lestranges, and his own wife was a daughter of Sir David Hanmer, an eminent lawyer and judge. He was the wealthiest member of what was left of the native Welsh aristocracy, with an annual income of about £200; in a poem in his praise Iolo Goch described his main residence at Sycharth.[2] According to tradition he spent some time as a young man at the Inns of Court in London studying law, but there is no conclusive proof of this. However, he certainly had some military

108

experience; in 1384 he was a member of the garrison of Berwick-upon-Tweed, serving under the command of his fellow-Welshman Sir Gregory Sais, and this was followed by participation in Richard II's Scottish campaign the following year.[3] He also served under Arundel in a naval campaign against the French in 1387. In 1386 he had appeared as a witness in the Scrope–Grosvenor case in the Court of Chivalry; Geoffrey Chaucer was a witness in the same action. But the most significant aspect of his background, especially in the light of what was to follow, was the fact that his mother was also a member of the native aristocracy; she was descended from the royal house of Deheubarth, so that in him the lines of Powys and Deheubarth met. This was to be of particular importance after the extinction of the Gwynedd line on the assassination of Owain ap Thomas ap Rhodri in 1378 and the death of Roger Mortimer, earl of March, in Ireland in 1398.

With such an ancestry and standing, as he did, at the centre of a closely-related network of leading Welsh families, among them the senior line of the descendants of Ednyfed Fychan, Owain was the obvious leader of a revolt, should one occur.[4] Several poems composed to him before the revolt exist; in one of them Iolo Goch very significantly stressed his descent and another poet, Gruffydd Llwyd, complained that, unlike three of his prominent Welsh contemporaries, he had not received the knighthood he merited.[5] Although he was not one of the obvious leaders of the native community and seems to have held no local offices, his ancestry gave him a unique status. He was also very much aware of the Welsh messianic and prophetic tradition and he and his advisers made use of it; a certain Crach Ffinnant, described as his 'prophet', was present at his proclamation and had earlier served with him in the Berwick garrison. The prophetic tradition formed part of his appeal to history in the letters he addressed to the king of Scots and the Irish lords seeking support at the beginning of the revolt and at one point he consulted one Hopcyn ap Thomas of Ynystawe in the lordship of Gower, known as an expert on prophecy.[6] If his movement was to make any headway it had to be associated with this tradition; Owain had to project himself as the *mab darogan* or son of prophecy in whom the prophecies were to be fulfilled. This was powerful political propaganda and it has to be understood in order to understand the revolt; it was part of the burgeoning awareness of a distinct nationality. This prophetic element is brought out by Shakespeare in his not unsympathetic portrayal of Owain in *King Henry IV, Part I*. He had inherited the mantle of Owain ap Thomas ap Rhodri as the *mab darogan*; indeed, a French chronicler commented that the earlier Owain had paved the way for him.[7]

Owain Glyn Dŵr, descended from the dynasties of Powys and Deheubarth, was therefore the obvious leader of a Welsh revolt. But why did this revolt erupt in 1400? This was an age of popular revolts all over Europe; between about 1350 and 1450 most countries, from Catalonia to Finland, experienced at least one.[8] The plague had led to a climate of restlessness and disorientation and this often led in turn to social protest in a world which seemed to have been turned upside-down. Many revolts were protests by the poor and the unfree against the social order; in England the Peasants' Revolt of 1381 was sparked off by the poll taxes of 1377, 1379 and 1381. Wales was subject to the same problems and pressures as the rest of Europe and the last two decades of the fourteenth century seem to have been a time of particular hardship. Much seigneurial income had come from the unfree and, although their number had diminished substantially, the same sums were still being demanded. But the English revolt had no impact on Wales, nor is there any evidence of that religious and millenarian ferment which was so common elsewhere; in Wales the existing vaticinatory and millenarian tradition was directed to political ends, first in the cause of Owain ap Thomas ap Rhodri and later in that of Owain Glyn Dŵr. Later still it was to be harnessed by the supporters of Henry Tudor. The Glyn Dŵr revolt was many things; its motivation was political and it was the work of the haves rather than of the have-nots. It was a massive protest by the political nation, a bid for political independence and, to some degree, a civil war. Its European parallels are to be found in

Bohemia, where religious dissent was transformed into national protest, and in Sweden, where a peasant revolt grew into a national rebellion against the Danish crown, rather than in England or in France. In Wales the revolt became a national rising, but it was one which had been planned and organised by the *uchelwyr*. A rising on this scale was able to subsume very real popular grievances and the leaders of the native community were able to contain and channel the stream of popular protest. Whether or not those who planned the revolt had intended it to go as far as it did is another question; like all such movements it probably acquired a momentum of its own as the prospect of a revived Welsh principality became a real possibility.

The traditional cause of the revolt was a boundary dispute between Owain and his neighbour Reginald de Grey, lord of Dyffryn Clwyd; Grey, it was alleged, had then withheld a summons to Owain for military service.[9] Although one contemporary chronicler gives this as the reason, it is not easy to accept it; a dispute with a neighbour might lead to a violent response, but the public proclamation of Owain as prince of Wales meant that his movement was a great deal more than a marcher quarrel. It is more likely that the leaders of the Welsh community had been planning a revolt for some time; a key part may have been played by the senior line of the descendants of Ednyfed Fychan, the sons of Tudur ap Goronwy of Penmynydd in Anglesey. If this were the case, Owain Glyn Dŵr was the obvious leader for such a movement and the poetry to him may be significant in this respect, particularly Iolo Goch's account of his ancestry; this poem may have been intended to remind him of who he was and where his duty lay. If the revolt had been planned in advance, the time had to be carefully chosen. Richard II had been deposed in 1399; it has sometimes been suggested that he had been popular in Wales and that his deposition had contributed to the revolt. There is, however, no evidence of any particular Welsh loyalty to Richard; indeed, he had seen the royal lands in Wales as nothing more than a source of patronage. His power-base had been Cheshire, which he had raised to the status of a principality. There was a rising in support of him in

Cheshire in 1400 and this may have suggested that the time was ripe for action in Wales.

The proclamation at Glyndyfrdwy was followed by an attack on Ruthin and subsequently on other towns in the north-east. A few days later the rebels were defeated by a Shropshire force, although there was a simultaneous rising in Anglesey led by Gwilym and Rhys ap Tudur ap Goronwy. Henry IV's response was to lead an army into north Wales; most of the rebels submitted and were pardoned. Owain meanwhile had disappeared and his lands were confiscated. The revolt seemed to be over; early in 1401 parliament enacted a series of penal statutes which laid a number of disabilities on the Welsh.[10] These restrictions were not, in fact, new; the statutes were in large part a repetition of a series of ordinances promulgated after the revolt of Madog ap Llywelyn at the end of the thirteenth century but ignored since then.[11] But they now caused considerable outrage, especially since so many had made their peace. On Good Friday 1401 Gwilym and Rhys ap Tudur captured Conwy castle by the simple expedient of occupying it while the garrison was in church.[12] This may have been no more than a protest at their having been excluded from the royal pardon and the return of the castle was soon negotiated, but the episode showed that the Welsh problem had not been solved. Owain now reappeared and defeated a royal force at Mynydd Hyddgen in northern Cardiganshire; a further royal campaign in the autumn of 1401 was a complete failure because Owain refused to give battle and the king withdrew after sacking the abbey of Strata Florida.

Owain's position was now growing stronger. In 1402 he captured Reginald de Grey and held him to ransom. He also captured Edmund Mortimer, a closer relative of Richard II than Henry IV, who was seen by some in England as Richard's legitimate successor. There was no question of the king's ransoming Mortimer, who was a potential focus of opposition in England, and he was to marry one of Owain's daughters. Once again Henry planned a campaign, this time to deal with Owain once and for all. Three armies were to follow the strategy which had proved so successful for Edward I, but they were all driven back by bad weather; there were many in England who were convinced that Owain was a magician who could control the elements. In the same year a further group of penal statutes was passed, aimed not only at the Welsh but also at Englishmen married to Welsh wives.[13] The justiciar of north Wales at this time was Henry Percy, known as Hotspur, the son of the earl of Northumberland. He had grievances of his own and in 1403 he rose in revolt; there is evidence of contact with some of Owain's leading supporters but none of actual collusion.[14] The Welsh of Flintshire, hitherto quiescent, rose with Hotspur and thus came into the revolt. Henry IV moved quickly; Hotspur and many of his supporters were defeated and killed at Shrewsbury, but this had no effect on the Welsh. Yet another royal campaign in south Wales was as fruitless as its predecessors had been, while Owain went on advancing, capturing castles and burning the town of Cardiff. Like the thirteenth-century princes, one of the secrets of his success was his mobility; he could appear without warning in any part of Wales. The following year he captured the royal castles of Harlech and Aberystwyth, which indicates that his army had an effective artillery train. He was, in fact, a great deal more than a successful guerilla leader, being able, as he was, to draw on a substantial reservoir of Welsh professional military experience which had seen service in France and Scotland. Harlech became his headquarters and he also summoned a Welsh parliament, attended by envoys from France and Castile, to Machynlleth in Powys.

By this time the revolt was acquiring an aura of success and Owain was now joined by some of the leading Welsh clerics who had prospered outside Wales, in particular the bishops of St Asaph and Bangor, John Trefor and Lewis Byford, and the archdeacon of Merioneth, Gruffydd Young; Young became his chancellor.[15] This accession of experienced canon lawyers and men of affairs provided the movement with that political and diplomatic expertise which was essential if a Welsh state was to be created; these were the kind of men who could provide such a state with its bureaucratic infrastructure. Owain's prime need, if the momentum was to be maintained, was for outside assistance and the obvious source of this was France. There had already been some naval assistance, but an embassy was now sent to the French court and the result, on 14 July 1404, was a treaty of alliance between King Charles VI and Owain, prince of Wales.[16] The following year saw negotiations with opponents of Henry IV in England and these culminated in the Tripartite Indenture, under the terms of which Owain was to have a much-expanded Wales, the earl of Northumberland was to control England north of the Trent and Edmund Mortimer's nephew was to become king.[17]

But the Tripartite Indenture never took effect and by now there were signs that the tide was beginning to turn. Owain suffered two military defeats in Gwent and in the second one at Pwll Melyn his brother Tudur was killed and one of his sons captured. However, the French alliance did produce some results; in the summer of 1405 a French force landed at Milford Haven, joined up with Owain and took Haverfordwest and Carmarthen. The combined forces then moved east, crossed the English border and reached Woodbury Hill near Worcester. This could have been a decisive stroke; the road to London lay open and the French saw an opportunity of toppling Henry IV. But Owain now decided to withdraw; he may have come to the conclusion that participation in the long-running Anglo-French struggle was no part of his strategy and he may also have realised that any further advance would have been into hostile territory with his lines of communication dangerously over-extended. A later parallel may be the withdrawal of Charles Edward Stuart from Derby in 1745. The failure to advance further into England may, perhaps, have been the beginning of the end, although yet another royal expedition ended in failure, driven back by the weather and its supplies ransacked. By early 1406 the French had departed, but this was not the end of the alliance. This was the period of the papal schism and as part of the province of Canterbury the Welsh church had recognised the Roman pope; now, following a meeting at Pennal near Machynlleth, Owain and his advisers set out their terms for transferring the spiritual allegiance of Wales to the rival pope at

Avignon, who was supported by France.[18] Among these terms were an independent Welsh ecclesiastical province, including some English dioceses and with an archbishop at St David's. Only Welsh-speaking clerics were to be appointed to Welsh benefices and two universities would be established, one in the north and one in the south.

The Pennal letter, almost certainly the work of Owain's clerical advisers, came too late. In 1405 an army from Dublin had restored order in Anglesey and from 1406 whole communities had begun to make their peace with the crown and to pay substantial fines for forgiveness. A faction favouring peace came to power in France and and Henry IV's position in England was becoming stronger. The earl of Northumberland rebelled and in 1408 he was defeated and killed at Bramham Moor; in the same year Harlech and Aberystwyth fell to royal armies and Owain's family was captured. The last raid on the English border was in 1410, when three of his leading lieutenants were captured and executed. Owain himself disappeared from view; he was offered a pardon by Henry V but there was no response and he may have died in 1415.[19] The revolt may be said to have ended in 1421 when his son Maredudd finally accepted a pardon.

The revolt of Owain Glyn Dŵr was, in the end, a failure. It failed because Wales had fought itself to a standstill in a war of attrition; in the end the superior power and resources of the English crown prevailed and French aid was too little and too late. Perhaps failure was inevitable and the revolt may be described as 'the massive protest of a conquered people'; perhaps Owain was too late in the light of what had happened in 1282.[20] The restoration of order took some time; substantial garrisons were maintained in mid-Wales for several years and there was continued unrest in Caernarfonshire and Merioneth as Maredudd tried to carry on the fight.[21] There was a fear that the Lollard leader Sir John Oldcastle was in league with the rebels; Oldcastle was, in fact, finally captured in Powys in 1417. There were few reprisals after the revolt, although the leaders of the 1410 raid and several others were executed. When Harlech surrendered in 1408 the terms included the retention of the defenders' lands and most former rebels or their sons recovered theirs. In 1413 the three counties of north Wales made fine of 1,600 marks for a communal pardon; in the same year all pre-1411 arrears from the northern principality were cancelled and an official enquiry led to the dismissal of Thomas Barneby, the chamberlain of north Wales, whose conduct had been, to say the least, equivocal.[22] Grants were even made for the replacement of livestock; Henry V, planning a military campaign in France and concerned about the possible threat of a Lollard rising, was disposed to be conciliatory. By the second decade of the century many were back in the offices which they had held before the revolt; royal and marcher authorities knew very well that Wales could not be governed without the cooperation and participation of the leaders of the native community and those who survived usually regained their lands and positions.

The penal statutes did leave their mark. Some new borough charters, like those of Brecon and Welshpool, did exclude Welsh burgesses and in 1433 Owain's son-in-law Sir John Scudamore was dismissed as deputy-justiciar of south Wales, despite a long record of loyal service to the crown, but this was due to the machinations of Edmund Beaufort; the episode does, however, show that the statutes could be used in the pursuit of personal rivalries and local disputes.[23] They were confirmed from time to time during the century and the burgesses of the castle boroughs of north Wales called for their enforcement on several occasions. But they were largely a dead letter, although they were not finally repealed until 1624. Nevertheless, there were grants of denizenship or English legal status to individuals like David Holbache of Oswestry, the first Welshman to sit in parliament, the London merchant Sir Lewis John from Carmarthenshire, who became a prominent landowner in Essex and a member of the king's council, and several military leaders.[24] Gwilym ap Gruffydd of Penrhyn in Caernarfonshire, a descendant of Ednyfed Fychan, petitioned for denizenship, claiming that all his ancestors had been English.[25]

The economic effects of the revolt were disastrous in the short term. For several years little revenue was collected from the principality or the march although it must be suspected that much that was uncollected found its way to Owain. There was widespread destruction, even of churches; the cathedrals at Bangor and St Asaph were both badly damaged. Many towns suffered; Carmarthen was sacked, Cardiff burned and the burgesses of Conwy claimed that over £5,000 worth of damage had been done.[26] But the long-term effects may be exaggerated; there is no lack of evidence in subsequent accounts of the flight of bondmen, the abandonment of communities and derelict mills and all these have often been seen as consequences of the revolt, but the origins of all of them are to be found in the years before 1400. They were, in reality, the result of the plague and the long-drawn-out crisis which followed it, although all these problems were aggravated by the revolt. In any case, an economy based on agriculture was able to recover far more rapidly than a modern industrial one would have done. The aim of the authorities in both the principality and the march was to try to encourage economic recovery and thus to restore revenues to their previous levels; there was some success in the short term but the underlying problems were not solved. Among individuals there were gainers and losers; in north Wales the senior line of the descendants of Ednyfed, who had played a key part in the revolt from the beginning, lost everything, although the great-grandson of one of the sons of Tudur ap Goronwy of Penmynydd was to conquer new worlds in 1485. But their kinsman Gwilym ap Gruffydd, who had also joined the revolt but who had made his peace with the authorities at an early stage, was able to acquire most of their lands and to found the family which was to dominate the northern principality until the middle of the next century.

New Horizons

The conclusion of the Glyn Dŵr revolt marks both an end and a beginning; in the words of one historian, 'Modern Wales . . . really begins in 1410'.[27] National awareness was strengthened;

117

for the first time most of Wales acted together and at the height of his power Owain controlled more of Wales than Llywelyn ap Gruffydd had ever done. Not everyone supported him; there was, as has already been mentioned, an element of civil war in the revolt. Two local squires died defending Caernarfon castle against the rebels and many leaders in the south remained loyal to the crown. One consequence was the strengthening of the power of the *uchelwyr* at the local level; those who had been involved in the revolt had managed to extricate themselves without too much trouble. They were now to move gradually on to a wider political stage and some were to become involved in the affairs of the kingdom. Another result was a steady decline in standards of public order; it could be said that order was not really restored in Wales until after 1536 because local leaders were too powerful and neither royal nor marcher authorities were ever again to be strong enough to impose their will. Under a strong king like Henry V royal government was effective and efficient and the quality of his officials was high, but his death in 1422 was followed by the long minority of Henry VI and the beginning of a steady process of deterioration. In the last resort only the crown could ensure order and the crown was weak; Henry VI's assumption of personal power in 1437 led to the massive misuse of royal patronage in the principality with even local offices, which local leaders regarded as their right, being bestowed on members of the royal household.[28] The appointment of magnates with many other interests as justiciars, such as the king's uncle Humphrey, duke of Gloucester, in north Wales in 1427 and south Wales in 1440, and the earl of Suffolk in south Wales in 1438 and north Wales in 1440 meant a lack of effective supervision from the top. The result was that the leaders of local communities could do more or less as they pleased; perhaps the most blatant example of these local bosses was Gruffydd ap Nicholas of Dinefwr in Carmarthenshire, who appears for the first time as deputy-justiciar of south Wales in 1437.[29] In the 1440s and 1450s Gruffydd was the effective ruler of the southern principality and, with the aid of his sons, he ran it as if it were his own private lordship, taking full advantage of the factional rivalry which was so evident at the heart of government. A similar part was played in the south-east by Sir William ap Thomas of Raglan and subsequently by his son William Herbert, while in the northern principality power passed into the hands of members of the royal household, in particular those who came from Cheshire.[30]

Men like Gruffydd ap Nicholas were a symptom rather than a cause of the contemporary malaise. Effective government needed supervision at the centre and responsible behaviour by the leaders of local communities and neither were forthcoming. After 1413 there was no prince of Wales of full age and most marcher lords were by now absentee magnates; in the march there was no substitute for supervision by a vigorous resident lord. Likewise in the principality magnate justiciars were generally absent and rule was through local deputies of whom Gruffydd ap Nicholas was only the most notorious. Such men had their own personal ambitions and struggles for local power and influence could often amount to private wars. Disorder was widespread; a power struggle in Cardiganshire in 1439 was won by one of the sons of Gruffydd ap Nicholas and there was extensive violence in the south-west in the 1440s and 1450s.[31] A graphic picture of disorder and savage family rivalry in Eifionydd in southern Caernarfonshire was drawn by Sir John Wynn of Gwydir in his history of his family written at the end of the sixteenth century.[32] In the county of Merioneth, described by one historian as 'ungoverned and ungovernable', there seems to have been a complete collapse of order and government in the 1450s and the Conwy valley, to which Sir John Wynn's ancestor moved, was the haunt of outlaws, among them the notorious Dafydd ap Siencyn.[33] One practice, common in the march and the southern principality, was the redemption of the great sessions. Following an announcement that such sessions were to be held, the leaders of the community concerned would offer a lump sum roughly equal to the income likely to be generated. The offer would be accepted and the sessions cancelled. In Brecon in 1418–19 the sessions were redeemed for 2,000 marks and in Newport in 1476 for 650 marks.[34] In Carmarthenshire between 1422 and 1485 only twelve out of 52 sessions ran their full course without being redeemed.[35]

But the breakdown of order in Wales can be exaggerated; the situation was no worse than it was in many parts of contemporary England where local rivalries were no less common. The causes in both countries were the same, among them being the increasing weakness of central government, the strains of an unwinnable war in France, the growth of factions and, after 1453, the intermittent insanity of the king. Courts went on being held and there is no record of any redemption of the sessions in the northern principality. Nor were individual marcher lordships self-contained havens of lawlessness; there had always been agreements between lordships for the extradition and even the punishment of felons and for hot pursuit. Days of the March or formal meetings on the common border for the settlement of disputes were an old-established practice and they continued to be held and often resulted in agreements or *cydfodau*.[36] Sessions which were redeemed might often be no more than devices for raising money or a crude form of taxation; there were perfectly adequate courts in both the principality and the march and redemption had gone on before 1400.

The power and influence of the *uchelwyr* were based on the holding of office and on the steady accumulation of land. The process of estate-building which began in the fourteenth century was now gathering momentum as the leaders of the community emerged from the revolt in an even stronger position; the outstanding example in north Wales was the Griffith family of Penrhyn, near Bangor. Gwilym ap Gruffydd, who had already acquired the seat of the senior line of the descendants of Ednyfed Fychan at Penmynydd by his first marriage, made his peace with the authorities in 1405 and was able to buy up other lands in Anglesey and Caernarfonshire. His second marriage to one of the Stanleys, a leading Cheshire family, gave him a new status and by the time he died in 1431 he was probably the richest man in north Wales.[37] Part of his wealth seems to have come from extensive business activity; according to a recently discovered list of his debtors compiled in 1406, he was dealing in wine, lending money, hiring out oxen and cattle and buying up tithes.[38] This is, unfortunately, the only document of its kind; it would be interesting to know how far other *uchelwyr* made money from trade and were thus enabled to buy more land. Gwilym's son Gwilym Fychan or William Griffith I went on building up the estate; he also created a further estate, that of Plas Newydd in Anglesey, for one of his illegitimate sons.[39] By the time he died in 1483 he dominated the principality of north Wales and the family continued to do so until 1540. Another northern example is the family of Bulkeley of Beaumaris.[40] William Bulkeley the elder came to Anglesey from Cheshire and married the daughter of Gwilym ap Gruffydd. The couple set about buying lands in Anglesey and Caernarfonshire and their son married the daughter and heiress of Bartholomew de Bolde, a Conwy burgess who had built up a substantial estate in the Conwy valley by purchase. The Bulkeley estate became one of the largest in north Wales and the early sixteenth century was to see a power struggle between the Bulkeleys and the Griffiths of Penrhyn. These were not the only new estates and marriage could play as significant a part as the burgeoning land market; the Mostyn family, with lands all over north Wales, owed its rise to a series of marriages in the fourteenth and fifteenth centuries.[41] Deeds in collections of family papers often chronicle the rise of these families; other examples are Clenennau in Caernarfonshire, Peniarth in Merioneth and Rhydodyn in Carmarthenshire. Nor was Gruffydd ap Nicholas found wanting; his grandson Sir Rhys ap Thomas would dominate the southern principality as the house of Penrhyn did the north.[42]

Wales was coming to play an increasing part in English politics. One reason for this was the increasing concentration of power in the march in magnate hands. The Duchy of Lancaster lordships, among them Kidwelly and Monmouth, had come into the possession of the crown on the accession of Henry IV in 1399. The largest marcher holding was the massive bloc of Mortimer lordships in mid-Wales; these were worth over £2,000 annually and in 1425 they were inherited by Richard Plantagenet, duke of York, through his mother, the Mortimer heiress. In the circumstances it was hardly surprising that Wales should have become involved in the dynastic struggle between York and Lancaster and that it should have been brought into the political mainstream. Both factions had power-bases in Wales; the principality and the Duchy lordships were largely Lancastrian in their sympathies, while the former Mortimer lordships were Yorkist, but there were exceptions on both sides. On the whole, local leaders tended to follow their lords, but loyalties might be dictated by local rivalries or even by the sides taken by particular families in the Glyn Dŵr revolt. There was also a degree of personal convenience; Gruffydd ap Nicholas, for example, was loyal to Lancaster and Henry VI as long as he was left in undisputed control of the south-west. When the king's half-brother Edmund Tudor was sent to restore order in south Wales in 1455 he was not welcomed by Gruffydd and before long the two were more or less at war. Edmund's capture of Carmarthen alarmed Richard of York, who was at that time in control of the kingdom, and the leading Welsh Yorkist, William Herbert, led a force into Wales and captured Edmund, who died soon afterwards; his place as leader of the Lancastrian party in the southern principality was taken by his brother Jasper. The northern principality was loyal to the king; when York had landed at Beaumaris in 1450 on his return from Ireland to make his first bid for power, William Griffith and William Bulkeley had been among those ordered to stop him.[43]

The civil war, which had begun with the first battle of St Albans in 1455, reached the Welsh border in 1459 with the Yorkist victory at Blore Heath and the Lancastrian one at Ludford Bridge.[44] The subsequent Yorkist victory at Mortimer's Cross near Leominster in 1461 was part of the sequence of events which brought York's son to the throne as Edward IV later in the same year and this in turn led to the mopping-up of Lancastrian resistance in Wales. The task was entrusted to William Herbert, appointed justiciar of south Wales for life in 1461 and of north Wales in 1467; after the fall of Pembroke and Tenby Jasper Tudor fled to Ireland. In 1468 he returned to north Wales and Herbert led a further campaign to deal with him once and for all; this led to the surrender of the last Lancastrian garrison at Harlech and this event really marks the end of the war in Wales. Next to Owain Glyn Dŵr, Herbert was the outstanding Welsh figure of the fifteenth century. He was the first Welshman to be ennobled, being created earl of Pembroke in 1468, and was close to Edward IV; one contemporary poet described him as 'King Edward's master-lock'.[45] The part he played in Wales marks a new departure; from now on the king would leave his Welsh lands and interests in the care of a trusted and experienced servant. Like most contemporary military commanders he was ruthless and he and his men were much feared in England. But in his own country he was admired and respected; the poet Guto'r Glyn called on him to expel the English and unite Wales.[46] His career shows how an *uchelwr* could now prosper on the English political stage; he was the virtual viceroy of Wales and at the same time he was a patron of the poets who were always welcome at Raglan. But his rise made him many enemies, particularly the earl of Warwick, who was also a marcher lord. Warwick rebelled in 1469 and this led to the defeat and execution of Herbert at Edgecote near Banbury; his death was seen by the poets as a national disaster for Wales. His place as royal representative was taken by the king's brother Richard, duke of Gloucester.

William Herbert was not the only *uchelwr* to make a distinguished career outside Wales in the fifteenth century; another example was Sir John Dwnn of Kidwelly in Carmarthenshire.[47] His great-grandfather Henry Dwnn had been an active supporter of Owain Glyn Dŵr and his father Gruffydd also took part in the revolt in his youth. Gruffydd subsequently served the crown in Wales and in France; he married a grand-daughter of Owain Glyn Dŵr and his sister was the wife of Gruffydd ap Nicholas. John held various offices and acquired lands in England. He was knighted in 1471 and carried out several diplomatic missions for Henry VII; he also commissioned a triptych, now in the National Gallery, from Hans Memlinc. Men like Herbert and Dwnn show that new doors of opportunity were opening for Welshmen, even before 1485, and that the Glyn Dŵr revolt had not stood in the way of the further rise of the leaders of the native community. Some of them, like Gruffydd Dwnn, Sir Richard Gethin of Builth and the outstanding Welsh captain of the time, Matthew Gough, distinguished themselves in the French wars and were rewarded with lands in Normandy, but these had all been lost to the resurgent French monarchy by 1450. There are many references to their military exploits by the poets, one of whom, Guto'r Glyn, may actually have served in France himself.[48]

Henry Tudor

Warwick's revolt led in 1471 to the temporary restoration of Henry VI and the flight of Edward IV, but Edward soon returned and at Tewkesbury in the same year the Lancastrian cause was destroyed once and for all. Henry's only son was killed in the battle and Henry died, probably murdered, a few days later. For Wales Tewkesbury was probably the most significant battle of the civil war because it ended the direct Lancastrian line and thus created an entirely new dynastic situation. Following the battle Jasper Tudor fled to Brittany with his young nephew Henry, the son of Edmund.[49] With the extinction of the house of Lancaster the young Henry Tudor was the nearest there was to a Lancastrian candidate for the crown; his mother Margaret Beaufort was a great-granddaughter of John of Gaunt. On his father's side he was descended from Ednyfed Fychan and the lineage which had played so significant a part in the northern principality until the Glyn Dŵr revolt. One of the five sons of Tudur ap Goronwy, Maredudd, had been involved in the revolt; he then disappears without trace from the historical record but his son Owen Tudor served the crown in France and then at court. His story is one of the great romances of history; he married Katherine of Valois, the widow of Henry V and mother of Henry VI, and they had three sons, Edmund, Jasper and Owen (who became a monk and died in 1501). Owen Tudor was executed after the battle of Mortimer's Cross, but Henry VI had showed great favour to his half-brothers, creating Edmund earl of Richmond and Jasper earl of Pembroke; Edmund had died in 1456 and Henry was born posthumously. As a child he had been in the custody of William Herbert at Raglan and Herbert may have intended to marry him to his daughter; after Herbert's death Jasper took care of him.

Jasper Tudor was the archetypal conspirator. He was now the effective leader of the Lancastrian party and from Brittany he maintained contact with Lancastrian supporters in Wales, paying clandestine visits from time to time and planning for the future, but the Yorkist hold seemed unassailable. Then, in 1483, Edward IV died suddenly, leaving his young son as his successor. Richard, duke of Gloucester, was appointed regent; his seizure of the throne and the disappearance of Edward V and his brother later the same year changed the situation entirely. The revolt of the duke of Buckingham drew no support in Wales, where he was an unpopular marcher lord; the Lancastrian cause revived and Jasper's conspiratorial activities now began to bear fruit. In Wales many of the poets were working for Henry Tudor, who had enough Welsh blood to make him a credible son of prophecy; the tradition of vaticinatory poetry was being harnessed to his cause, with Henry being hailed as the Swallow or the Bull. Poets such as Dafydd Llwyd looked forward to a *'haf hir felyn'* ('long golden summer') when the son of prophecy would come into his own.[50] Henry was praised and Richard denounced; some poets actually accused the latter of mistreating his nephews and in some of the poetry there is a pronounced anti-English note.[51] Opponents of Richard were now making their way to Brittany to join Henry and Margaret Beaufort began discussions with Edward IV's widow Elizabeth Woodville with a view to arranging a marriage between her son and Edward's daughter Elizabeth. After an abortive expedition in 1483 pressure by Richard III on the duke of Brittany forced Jasper and Henry to seek refuge in France, where an invasion was planned; warning letters were sent to supporters in Wales whom Jasper had long been cultivating, promising to release them from their 'miserable servitudes'.[52] Early in August 1485 Henry, at the head of a force of French mercenaries and English exiles, landed at Mill Bay on Milford Haven and began his advance through Wales.[53] On the way he was joined by a number of those with whom Jasper had been in contact; the most important of these was probably Gruffydd ap Nicholas's grandson Rhys ap Thomas of Dinefwr, now the dominant figure in the south-west. The army moved through mid-Wales to Shrewsbury and then into the English midlands. At Bosworth near Leicester on 22 August contact was made with Richard III and his army and Henry's victory was secured when his stepfather Lord Stanley and his brother Sir William, who had been biding their time, joined him. Richard was killed and the penniless exile Henry Tudor became King Henry VII.

For Wales it was the psychological rather than the practical effects of Bosworth which were important. The impact on the national imagination was stupendous and this can clearly be seen in the response of the poets. The son of prophecy had returned to his people and Llywelyn ap Gruffydd had been avenged. The descendant of Ednyfed Fychan wore the English crown; it was, in a sense, the apotheosis of the *uchelwyr*. At Bosworth Henry had fought under the banner of the red dragon and this somehow made it a Welsh victory. But how Welsh was Henry Tudor? Only one of his four grandparents was Welsh; he also had English, French and, through the mother of Katherine of Valois, German blood. However, his descent from a lineage as eminent as that of Ednyfed Fychan meant that he stood at the centre of an extensive network of kinsmen, especially in north Wales. Men like William Griffith II of Penrhyn were distant relatives and his great-great-grandfather Dafydd Fychan ap Dafydd Llwyd of Trefeilir in Anglesey somehow symbolises his standing. Dafydd was an *uchelwr* of the second rank who held no more than local office, but the marriages of his seven daughters, one of them to Maredudd ap Tudur, contributed to that web of family connections which gave Henry credibility in the eyes of the leaders of the native community and drew them to his cause.[54] The fact that he had spent part of his childhood at Raglan may have meant that he could speak Welsh and he is said to have enjoyed Welsh poetry.[55] The red dragon became one of the supporters of the royal arms and his first-born son was christened Arthur, an obvious appeal to history, albeit the mythical version. Throughout the sixteenth century he was seen as the liberator of the Welsh; George Owen of Henllys, the Pembrokeshire antiquary, described him as 'the Moses who delivered us from bondage'.[56] No other Welshman, apart, perhaps, from David Lloyd George, was to achieve so much.

Henry knew very well how much he owed to the support of Welshmen and many were rewarded. His greatest debt was to his uncle Jasper, who had kept the flame alive; he was created duke of Bedford and given the oversight of Wales and the marches, although with nothing like the power that William Herbert had enjoyed under Edward IV. Rhys ap Thomas was knighted and in 1496 he was appointed justiciar of south Wales. But the new king was not prepared to bestow too much power on any individual; all grants of offices were made during his pleasure and not for life. Many who had fought at Bosworth were rewarded with lesser offices; loyalty at every level was recognised.[57] There are some complaints from the poets after 1485 that Henry had not done as much as he should for Wales and that Englishmen were preferred, but it is probably fair to say that they expected too much.[58] It is unlikely that their comments reflected the views of the leaders of the community; the change of regime had made no difference to their power and influence and they understood very well that the king's priorities were to restore stability, maintain order and remain on the throne. It was enough for them that he was there and he could rely on their support in putting down later risings. A Yorkist rising in the lordship of Brecon in 1486 was suppressed by Sir Rhys ap Thomas, who also fought for him at Stoke in 1487 and at Blackheath ten years later; in 1507 Sir Rhys organised a great tournament at his castle of Carew in Pembrokeshire to symbolise the reconciliation of Wales and England.[59] But where the maintenance of order and stability were concerned, no past service, however great, could save anyone who plotted against him; in 1495 his stepfather's brother Sir William Stanley, who had helped to turn the tide at Bosworth in his favour, was executed for his part in the conspiracy of Perkin Warbeck.

What Henry VII did not do was to try and impose a final solution on Wales's administrative problems. In administrative terms Wales was an anomaly, with the long-standing division between principality and march making it impossible to legislate for the whole country. By 1485 most marcher lordships had come into the possession of the crown, the main exceptions being the lordships of the Stafford family, dukes of Buckingham, in the south-east and those of the Stanleys in the north-east. But there was no kind of central governmental machinery for the royal lordships; each one of them was still completely autonomous. The surviving lords were obliged to make formal agreements with the crown for the maintenance of order but the march remained a patchwork of separate jurisdictions. In 1471 Edward IV had made his son Edward prince of Wales and two years later had sent him to Ludlow with a council, entrusted with extensive powers, to supervise the principality and march in his name; in 1489 Henry did the same thing on the grant of the principality to his elder son Arthur and the council survived Arthur's death in 1502 to become, during the reign of Henry VIII, the Council in the Marches of Wales. Edward IV had also pioneered indentures of the march or formal agreements with marcher lords; what Henry now sought to do was to make the existing system work more efficiently by reviving some of the steps which his Yorkist predecessor had taken while at the same time strengthening the position of the crown.

The problems of governing Wales were as much financial as administrative and Henry was determined to put the finances of the crown on a sound footing. These problems went back to the second half of the fourteenth century and in the northern principality they were exacerbated by the collapse of revenue from bond townships, many of which had long since been abandoned by their inhabitants. Bond status was by now largely irrelevant and free tenants were moving into vacant bond lands. In 1490 steps were taken to recover as much revenue as possible; the chamberlain of north Wales, Sir William Griffith II of

Penrhyn, was dismissed and the financial administration at Caernarfon was taken over by royal officials whose task was to maximise the income from the principality.[60] The resultant financial demands led to new pressures on the community and one of the consequences was a rising in Merioneth in 1498 which led to the capture of Harlech castle by the rebels; troops had to be brought in to restore order and a heavy fine had to be paid to win back the king's goodwill.[61] There were similar problems in the march; like the king, the duke of Buckingham was anxious to gather the maximum revenue from his lordships, but in Brecon in 1496 arrears of £2,000 had to be written off.[62] Buckingham could not depend on the goodwill of his tenants; he was harsh and grasping and this made him as unpopular as his father had been. The only justification for bond status was the revenue which bondmen had generated and in the north steps were now taken to deal with the problem. There was a long-standing demand for enfranchisement and in 1447 the duke of York had freed the bondmen in his mid-Wales lordships of Ceri and Cydewain; now, in 1503, the community of the principality of north Wales paid £2,000 for a charter, granted in 1504, which repealed the Glyn Dŵr penal statutes and abolished partible succession to land (although this had long been ignored by those who were building up estates), along with various dues.[63] A further charter in 1507 abolished other servile dues and enfranchised royal and episcopal bondmen; the legal position of private bondmen remained uncertain.[64] Similar charters were granted to the communities of the lordships of Bromfield and Yale in 1505, Chirk and Denbigh in 1506 and Dyffryn Clwyd in 1508.[65] These charters were sometimes seen in the past as a consequence of Henry's great and abiding concern for the welfare of his fellow-countrymen; in actual fact they were far from being spontaneous expressions of royal generosity and were bought by their recipients. They were not welcomed by the northern castle boroughs, although there was a steadily increasing Welsh presence in them, and there was also some doubt as to their validity.[66]

It is easy to see fifteenth-century Wales as a hotbed of

lawlessness and disorder but, as in England, the impact of this can easily be exaggerated. There is some evidence of economic recovery after the revolt; the main exports of Wales were cattle and cloth and the latter had long since replaced the export of raw wool. The depopulation of bond townships had meant that an increasing amount of land was now given over to grazing and therefore to large-scale sheep-rearing, which was no longer a monastic and seigneurial monopoly. The most highly organised cloth industry was in and around Ruthin in the lordship of Dyffryn Clwyd; it is significant that the Grey family, lords of Dyffryn Clwyd since the Edwardian conquest, were usually resident in the lordship and it is no coincidence that it was capably and efficiently run. The evidence of contemporary poetry shows that there was no lack of visible wealth among the *uchelwyr* who were the patrons of the poetic tradition and some of whom were themselves poets. The period between 1450 and 1550 saw one of the great flowerings of Welsh poetry; this was when poets like Guto'r Glyn, Lewis Glyn Cothi, Dafydd Nanmor, Dafydd ab Edmwnd and Tudur Aled flourished and it was the patronage of the *uchelwyr*, from whose ranks many of them came, which sustained their art.[67] They gave voice to the social values of their society and in doing so they produced much great poetry. They were the poets of the Welsh political nation and their work can reveal much about contemporary political attitudes. Leaders like William Herbert and Gruffydd ap Nicholas were eminent patrons and in the early 1450s the latter is said to have presided over an *eisteddfod* at Carmarthen which revised the traditional metres. Patronage was a form of conspicuous consumption; so, too, was the construction of new and grander houses and surviving examples like Cochwillan near Bangor, the magnificent timber Bryndraenog in Radnor-shire and William Herbert's castle at Raglan bear witness to this.

The rebuilding and embellishment of churches is often an indicator of prosperity and there is no lack of examples from late fifteenth- and early sixteenth-century Wales. Town churches include Tenby and St John's in Cardiff; the splendid group of churches in the north-east, among them Wrexham, Mold and Gresford, owed much to the patronage of Henry VII's mother Margaret Beaufort, while collegiate churches like Clynnog Fawr in Caernarfonshire and Holyhead were rebuilt.[68] But it was not an age of profound religious devotion; on the eve of the Reformation most Welsh religious communities were moribund.[69] Abbots and many of the parish clergy came from *uchelwr* families; they were patrons of the poets, who describe a way of life which can only be described as extremely secular. Religion for many was a matter of habit, although pilgrimages to St David's or Bardsey, to the shrine of Dwynwen, patroness of lovers, at Llanddwyn in Anglesey, or even to Santiago de Compostella or Rome continued to be popular.[70] A good deal of religious poetry survives, but it does not usually reflect intense personal devotion, although there is a body of poetry from the early years of the century, attributed to Siôn Cent, which is rather more censorious and which reminds the *uchelwyr* in particular of the vanity of human wishes and aspirations and the imminence of the Day of Judgement.[71]

Henry VII died in 1509. He never had the opportunity to make a fresh start in Wales and it is doubtful if he had any wish to do so. Like Edward IV he had depended on men rather than institutions to govern the country and had put his trust in such local magnates as Sir Rhys ap Thomas. The new king Henry VIII had little interest in Wales, at least in the first part of his reign; Sir Rhys remained in control in the south until his death in 1525 and a similar part was played in the northern principality by Sir William Griffith III, the deputy to the absentee justiciar, the king's brother-in-law Charles Brandon, duke of Suffolk. Griffith ruled with a very heavy hand, claiming that local difficulties made this unavoidable.[72] Two prominent figures remained in the march; one was Charles Somerset, earl of Worcester, the illegitimate son of the third duke of Somerset and one of those who had landed with Henry Tudor in 1486. He had married the daughter and heiress of William Herbert's son, but most of what he had in the march he owed to royal favour and generosity and he behaved accordingly.[73] The other leading

131

marcher lord was the duke of Buckingham, who was rich, arrogant and unpopular. He had been on friendly terms with Henry VIII, but had offended Wolsey; Henry became increasingly suspicious of him, especially since he was a close enough relative to have an interest in the succession at a time when the king had no direct male heir. In due course Buckingham was accused of treason and in 1521 he was tried and executed. The fall of the last of the marcher magnates may be said to mark the end of an era and, indeed, the end of medieval Wales.

The fifteenth century began with a massive national revolt; it ended with a dynasty of Welsh extraction on the throne and a new self-confidence. Both the Glyn Dŵr revolt and Henry Tudor's victory at Bosworth had contributed to a burgeoning national awareness and the latter's effect on the Welsh psyche cannot be ignored, marking as it did the end of a sense of alienation. Welshmen had crossed the border to seek their fortunes before 1485, but the presence of a descendant of Anglesey *uchelwyr* on the throne somehow symbolised new opportunities, although it must be said that self-help often played as important a part as patronage in the rise of individuals. The next century was to see great and far-reaching changes in a Wales which was to experience the impact of Reformation, Renaissance and new political and administrative relationships. But history is as much about continuity as change and the origins of much that is seen as typical of Tudor Wales are to be found in the preceding centuries.

CONCLUSION

In the late summer of 1064 Earl Harold Godwinson brought a gift to King Edward the Confessor; it consisted of the figurehead of the ship of Gruffydd ap Llywelyn, king of Gwynedd, who had brought most of Wales under his rule, and the head of Gruffydd himself.[1] This macabre offering symbolised the end of a major threat to Harold's ambition to succeed to the English throne on the death of the childless king. Gruffydd's alliance with Earl Aelfgar of Mercia had imperilled the precarious balance of power in England and this had necessitated his destruction. On his death Welsh politics reverted to their usual pattern; Gwynedd and Powys passed to his half-brothers Bleddyn and Rhiwallon ap Cynfyn, while Deheubarth and Morgannwg were restored to their own dynasties and this was the situation when the Normans arrived. In 1297 a London goldsmith, Master John Pater Noster, in a petition to the king, referred to himself being in his forge, looking at the head of Llywelyn ap Gruffydd, still, after fifteen years, exposed on the Tower of London.[2] And on 17 May 1521 Edward Stafford, duke of Buckingham, the last great marcher magnate, met his end at the hands of the headsman.

Three severed heads may appear to be a bloodthirsty way of defining the history of medieval Wales, but these decapitations symbolise key points; the death of Harold Godwinson two years after Gruffydd secured the Norman conquest of England, with far-reaching consequences for Wales and the death of Llywelyn

133

ap Gruffydd meant the end of political independence, while the execution of Buckingham really marked the end of over four centuries of marcher lordship and set the scene for Thomas Cromwell's creation of a single, territorially-defined Wales. The history of medieval Wales sees a gradual transition from a multiplicity of kingdoms, through an attempt to create a single principality and a bid to recover the independence lost in 1282, to its integration in a state ruled by the descendants of a fourteenth-century burgess of the town of Newborough and an Anglesey squire. The middle ages saw the emergence of a national consciousness and sense of identity and the flowering of a literary culture which was to contribute, through the transla- tion of the scriptures and the Anglican liturgy, to the survival of the native language to the present day, a survival attested by some of the end-notes in this book.

The history of medieval Wales cannot, therefore, be ignored or dismissed as irrelevant. It is an integral part of the national experience and its imprint is visible to this day in the ruins of castles, both those of native rulers and invaders, in isolated country churches and in many Welsh towns. A walk on Newborough Warren in Anglesey is a reminder of the great storm of 1330. The coffin of Llywelyn ab Iorwerth can still be seen in Llanrwst church. And the linguistic frontier in Pembrokeshire still reflects the coming of Flemish settlers in 1108. In the seventeenth century a family near Grenoble in the French province of Dauphiné claimed, inaccurately, to be descended from Owain ap Thomas ap Rhodri, the last heir of the Gwynedd dynasty.[3] But the sons and grandsons of those who had followed Henry Tudor to Bosworth would sit in parliament and serve as justices of the peace; the Wales of 1521 was a very different place from that of 1064.

NOTES AND REFERENCES

Abbreviations

BBCS   *Bulletin of the Board of Celtic Studies*
CPR   *Calendar of the Patent Rolls*
EconHR   *Economic History Review*
EHR   *English Historical Review*
JMHRS   *Journal of the Merioneth Historical and Record Society*
NLWJ   *National Library of Wales Journal*
PBA   *Proceedings of the British Academy*
TAAS   *Transactions of the Anglesey Antiquarian Society*
TCHS   *Transactions of the Caernarvonshire Historical Society*
TDHS   *Transactions of the Denbighshire Historical Society*
THSC   *Transactions of the Honourable Society of Cymmrodorion*
TRHS   *Transactions of the Royal Historical Society*
WHR   *Welsh History Review*

INTRODUCTION

1. R. R. Davies, *Conquest, Coexistence and Change; Wales 1063–1415* (Oxford: Clarendon Press, 1987), p. viii.
2. Huw Pryce, *Native Law and the Church in Medieval Wales* (Oxford, Clarendon Press, 1993), p. 71.
3. Gwyn A. Williams, *When was Wales?* (Harmondsworth; Penguin Books, 1985), pp. 180–3; Dai Smith, *Wales! Wales?* (London: George Allen & Unwin, 1984), pp. 40–54; this view was not actually put forward by Professor Williams or Professor Smith, but

they were interpreted in this way by several commentators. An example of the second view is W. Ambrose Bebb, *Machlud yr Oesoedd Canol* (Swansea, Swansea Printers Ltd, 1951); see also the salutary comments of R. T. Jenkins, 'Yr apêl at hanes' in *Yr Apêl at Hanes* (Wrexham: Hughes a'i Fab, 1930), pp. 142–78.

1 OF HISTORY AND HISTORIANS

1. Geoffrey of Monmouth, *The History of the Kings of Britain*, ed. and trans. Lewis Thorpe (Harmondsworth: Penguin Books, 1966), p. 51.
2. Ibid., pp. 282–3.
3. Brynley F. Roberts, 'Historical writing' in A. O. H. Jarman and G. R. Hughes (eds), *A Guide to Welsh Literature* (Swansea: Christopher Davies, 1976), p. 245.
4. The three versions of *Brut y Tywysogyon* have been edited and translated by Thomas Jones (Cardiff: University of Wales Press, 1952, 1955, 1971); J. Beverley Smith, *The Sense of History in Medieval Wales* (University College of Wales, Aberystwyth, Inaugural Lecture, 1989), pp. 7–10.
5. Kathleen Hughes, *The Welsh Latin Chronicles, Annales Cambriae and related texts* (London: British Academy, 1974), pp. 11–28; Thomas Jones, 'Cronica de Wallia and other documents from Exeter Cathedral Library MS 3514', *BBCS*, 12 (1946), pp. 27–44; J. Williams ab Ithel (ed.), *Annales Cambriae* (London: Rolls Series, 1860).
6. 'O Oes Gwrtheyrn Gwrtheneu' in J. Rhŷs and J. Gwenogvryn Evans (eds), *The Text of the Bruts from the Red Book of Hergest* (Oxford: 1890), p. 404–6.
7. D. Simon Evans (ed.), *Historia Gruffud vab Kenan* (Cardiff: University of Wales Press, 1971). For an English translation see Arthur Jones (ed.), *History of Gruffydd ap Cynan* (Manchester University Press, 1910).
8. R. T. Gunther, *Early Science in Oxford 14: Life and Letters of Edward Lhwyd* (Oxford University Press, 1945), p. 371.
9. Roberts, 'Historical writing', pp. 246–7; Smith, *Sense of History*, pp. 7–8.
10. Adam of Usk, *Chronicon*, ed. E. Maunde Thompson, 2nd edn (London: Henry Frowde, 1904); J. E. Lloyd, *Owen Glendower* (Oxford University Press, 1931), pp. 147–54.
11. Lloyd, *Owen Glendower*, pp. 157–8.
12. Glanmor Williams, 'Some Protestant views of early British church

history' in *Welsh Reformation Essays* (Cardiff: University of Wales Press, 1967), pp. 207–17; *Episcopal Acts and cognate documents relating to Welsh sees, 1066–1272*, Vol. 1 (Cardiff: Historical Society of the Church in Wales, 1946), pp. 249–50.

13. Williams, 'Some Protestant views', pp. 212–3; Garfield H. Hughes (ed.), *Rhagymadroddion*, Cardiff: University of Wales Press, 1951), pp. 17–43.

14. Williams, 'Some Protestant views', pp. 208–14.

15. Henry Ellis (ed.), *Polydore Vergil's English History* (London: Camden Society, 1846); A. O. H. Jarman, 'Y ddadl ynghylch Sieffre o Fynwy', *Llên Cymru*, 2 (1952), pp. 5–6.

16. Gwyn A. Williams, *Madoc: the making of a myth* (London: Eyre Methuen, 1979), pp. 36–40.

17. Jarman, 'Y ddadl', p. 11; David Powel, *The Historie of Cambria now called Wales* (London: John Harding, 1811), p. xi.

18. B. G. Charles, *George Owen of Henllys* (Aberystwyth: National Library of Wales, 1977).

19. Sir John Wynn, *History of the Gwydir Family and Memoirs*, ed. J. Gwynfor Jones (Llandysul: Gomer Press, 1990).

20. M. Henry Jones, 'Wales and Hungary', *THSC* (1968), pp. 25–6.

21. T. Pennant, *A Tour in Wales*, Vol. 1 (London, 1784), reprinted with introduction by R. Paul Evans (Wrexham: Bridge Books, 1991), pp. 326–94.

22. Edward Owen, 'Owain Lawgoch – Yeuain de Galles', *THSC* (1899–1900), pp. 6–105.

23. Aneurin Owen (ed. and trans.) *Ancient Laws and Institutes of Wales*, (London: Record Commission, 1841); Henry Ellis (ed.), *Registrum vulgariter nuncupatum The Record of Caernarvon* (London: Record Commission, 1838).

24. J. E. Lloyd, 'Wales and the coming of the Normans', *THSC* (1899–1900), pp. 122–79; *A History of Wales from the earliest times to the Edwardian conquest*, 2 vols, (London: Longmans, 1911).

25. T. F. Tout, review in *EHR*, 17 (1912), pp. 132–5.

26. Thomas Richards, obituary, *TCHS*, 8 (1947), pp. 1–4.

27. E. A. Lewis, 'The decay of tribalism in north Wales', *THSC* (1902–3), pp. 1–75.

28. E. A. Lewis, *The Mediaeval Boroughs of Snowdonia* (London: Henry Sotheran, for the University of Wales, 1912); 'The development of industry and commerce in Wales during the middle ages', *TRHS*, 2nd series, 17 (1903), pp. 121–73; 'A contribution to the commercial history of medieval Wales', *Y Cymmrodor*, 24 (1913), pp. 86–188.

29. J. G. Edwards, 'Hywel Dda and the Welsh lawbooks', reprinted in D. Jenkins (ed.), *Celtic Law Papers introductory to Welsh medieval law and government* (Brussels: Les éditions de la librairie encyclopédique, 1973), pp. 137–60.

30. J. G. Edwards, *Littere Wallie preserved in Liber A in the Public Record Office* (Cardiff: University of Wales Press, 1940).

31. J. G. Edwards, 'Edward I's castle-building in north Wales', *PBA*, 32 (1950), pp. 15–81; 'The Normans and the Welsh march', *PBA*, 42 (1956), pp. 155–77.

32. J. G. Edwards, *The Principality of Wales 1267–1967* (Caernarfon: Caernarvonshire Historical Society, 1969).

33. William Rees, *South Wales and the March 1284–1415: a social and agrarian study* (Oxford University Press, 1924); Gwynedd O. Pierce, obituary, *WHR* 9 (1979), p. 488.

34. William Rees, 'The Black Death in Wales' in R. W. Southern (ed.), *Essays in Medieval History* (London: Macmillan, 1968), pp. 179–99.

35. William Rees, *Industry before the Industrial Revolution*, 2 vols (Cardiff: University of Wales Press, 1968); *Calendar of Ancient Petitions relating to Wales* (Cardiff: University of Wales Press, 1975).

36. T. Jones Pierce, 'The growth of commutation in Gwynedd during the thirteenth century', *BBCS*, 10 (1941), pp. 309–32; 'A Caernarvonshire manorial borough', *TCHS*, 3 (1941), pp. 3–32; 'The old borough of Nefyn 1355–1882', *TCHS*, 18 (1957), pp. 36–53.

37. T. Jones Pierce, 'The age of the princes' in D. M. Lloyd (ed.), *The Historical Basis of Welsh Nationalism* (Cardiff: Plaid Cymru, 1950), pp. 42–59.

38. T. Jones Pierce, 'The *gafael* in Bangor manuscript 1939', *THSC* 1942, pp. 158–88; J. Beverley Smith (ed.), *Medieval Welsh Society* (Cardiff: University of Wales Press, 1972).

39. Glyn Roberts, ' "Wyrion Eden": the Anglesey descendants of Ednyfed Fychan in the fourteenth century', *TAAS* 1951, pp. 34–72.

40. Glyn Roberts, 'Teulu Penmynydd', *THSC* 1959, pp. 9–37.

41. Glyn Roberts, *Aspects of Welsh History*, eds. A. H. Dodd and J. Gwynn Williams (Cardiff: University of Wales Press, 1969).

42. For Dafydd Jenkins's contributions see the bibliography in T. M. Charles-Edwards, Morfydd E. Owen and D. B. Walters (eds) *Lawyers and Laymen: studies in the history of law presented to Professor Dafydd Jenkins on his seventy-fifth birthday* (Cardiff: University of Wales Press, 1986); T. M. Charles-Edwards, *Early Irish and Welsh Kinship* (Oxford: Clarendon Press, 1993); Pryce, *Native Law and the Church in Medieval Wales.*

43. R. Ian Jack, *Medieval Wales* (London: The Sources of History, 1972), p. 233.
44. David Knowles, review, *History* 48 (1963), p. 360.
45. Wendy Davies, *The Llandaff Charters* (Aberystwyth: National Library of Wales, 1979).
46. Lynn H. Nelson, *The Normans in South Wales 1071–1170* (Austin: University of Texas Press, 1966); J. Le Patourel, *The Norman Empire* (Oxford: Clarendon Press, 1976); W. L. Warren, *Henry II* (London: Eyre Methuen, 1973), pp. 153–69.
47. R. R. Davies, 'Kings, lords and liberties in the march of Wales 1066–1272', *TRHS*, 5th series, 29 (1979), pp. 41–61.
48. David Walker, 'Gerald of Wales, Archdeacon of Brecon', in David Walker and O. W. Jones (eds), *Links with the Past: Swansea and Brecon historical essays* (Llandybie: Christopher Davies, 1974), pp. 67–87; 'Gerald of Wales: a review of recent work', *Journal of the Historical Society of the Church in Wales*, 24 (1974), pp. 13–26; Michael Richter, *Giraldus Cambrensis: the growth of the Welsh nation* (Aberystwyth: National Library of Wales, 1972); Robert Bartlett, *Gerald of Wales 1146–1223* (Oxford: Clarendon Press, 1982).
49. J. Beverley Smith, *Llywelyn ap Gruffudd, Tywysog Cymru* (Cardiff: University of Wales Press, 1986).
50. J. Beverley Smith, 'Gruffydd Llwyd and the Celtic alliance', *BBCS*, 26 (1976), pp. 463–78; 'Edward II and the allegiance of Wales', *WHR*, 8 (1976), pp. 139–71; 'Crown and community in the principality of north Wales in the reign of Henry Tudor', *WHR*, 3 (1966), pp. 145–71.
51. Keith Williams-Jones, *The Merioneth Lay Subsidy Roll 1292–93* (Cardiff: University of Wales Press, 1976), pp. vii–cxxxv.
52. Llinos Beverley Smith, 'The death of Llywelyn ap Gruffydd: the narratives reconsidered', *WHR*, 11 (1982), pp. 200–14; 'The *gravamina* of the community of Gwynedd against Llywelyn ap Gruffudd', *BBCS*, 31 (1984), pp. 158–76.
53. Ceri W. Lewis, 'The Treaty of Woodstock: its background and significance', *WHR*, 2 (1964), pp. 37–65; Gwyn A. Williams, 'The succession to Gwynedd, 1238–47', *BBCS*, 20 (1964), pp. 393–413.
54. R. R. Davies, 'Law and national identity in thirteenth-century Wales' in R. R. Davies, R. A. Griffiths, I. G. Jones and K. O. Morgan (eds) *Welsh Society and Nationhood: historical essays presented to Glanmor Williams* (Cardiff: University of Wales Press, 1984), pp. 51–69.
55. R. R. Davies, 'The twilight of Welsh law', *History*, 51 (1966), pp.

143–64; 'The survival of the bloodfeud in medieval Wales', *History*, 54 (1969), pp. 338–57.

56. R. R. Davies (ed.), *The British Isles 1100–1500: comparisons, contrasts and connections* (Edinburgh: John Donald, 1988).

57. J. F. Lydon, 'Lordship and crown: Llywelyn of Wales and O'Connor of Connacht', in Davies, *The British Isles*, pp. 48–63.

58. Ralph A. Griffiths, *The Principality of Wales in the Later Middle Ages: the structure and personnel of government, I South Wales, 1277–1536* (Cardiff: University of Wales Press, 1972).

59. R. R. Davies, 'Owain Glyn Dŵr and the Welsh squirearchy', *THSC* 1968 (ii), pp. 150–69.

60. J. E. Messham, 'The county of Flint and the rebellion of Owen Glyndwr in the records of the earldom of Chester', *Journal of the Flintshire Historical Society*, 23 (1967–8), pp. 1–34; R. K. Turvey, 'The marcher shire of Pembroke and the Glyndŵr rebellion', *WHR*, 15 (1990), pp. 151–68; Keith Williams-Jones, 'The taking of Conwy castle, 1401', *TCHS*, 30 (1978), pp. 7–43.

61. Ralph A. Griffiths, 'Wales and the marches', in S. B. Chrimes, C. D. Ross and R. A. Griffiths (eds) *Fifteenth-century Europe* (Manchester University Press: 1972), pp. 145–72; 'Patronage, politics and the principality of Wales 1413–1461' in H. Hearder and H. R. Loyn (eds) *British Government and Administration: studies presented to S. B. Chrimes* (Cardiff: University of Wales Press, 1974), pp. 69–86; 'Gentlemen and rebels in later medieval Cardiganshire', *Ceredigion* 5 (1964–5), pp. 143–67.

62. R. A. Griffiths (ed.), *Boroughs of Medieval Wales* (Cardiff: University of Wales Press, 1978); Ian Soulsby, *The Towns of Medieval Wales: a study in their history, archaeology and general topography* (Chichester: Phillimore, 1983).

63. H. E. Hallam (ed.), *The Agrarian History of England and Wales*, Vol. 2 (Cambridge University Press, 1988), pp. 260– 71, 412–96, 699– 714, 933–65, 998–1002; E. Miller (ed.), Vol. 3, (Cambridge University Press, 1991), pp. 92–106, 238–54, 648–61, 894–919. The contributions to Vol. 2 are by R. Ian Jack and L. A. S. Butler and those to Vol. 3 are by D. Huw Owen and L. A. S. Butler.

64. Edwards, *Littere Wallie*, pp. xxxvi–lxix.

65. J. Conway Davies, *The Welsh Assize Roll 1277–1284* (Cardiff: University of Wales Press, 1940), pp. 1–233.

66. F. M. Powicke, *King Henry III and the Lord Edward* (Oxford University Press, 1947), Vol. 2, pp. 618–85.

67. S. B. Chrimes, *King Edward I's Policy for Wales* (Cardiff: National Museum of Wales, 1969).

Notes and References

68. Davies, *Conquest, Coexistence and Change: Wales, 1063–1415*, p. 330.
69. See, for example, J. Beverley Smith, 'Llywelyn ap Gruffydd and the march of Wales', *Brycheiniog* 20 (1982–3), pp. 9–22.
70. Smith, *Llywelyn ap Gruffudd*, pp. 238–392.

2 THE NORMAN CHALLENGE

1. 1063 has usually been accepted as the date of Gruffydd ap Llywelyn's death, but Benjamin T. Hudson, 'The destruction of Gruffydd ap Llywelyn', *WHR*, 15 (1991), pp. 332–40, 348–50, argues convincingly for 1064.
2. Wendy Davies, *Patterns of Power in Early Wales* (Oxford: Clarendon Press, 1990), pp. 56–60.
3. Glyn Roberts, 'Wales on the eve of the Norman conquest', in *Aspects of Welsh History*, p. 275.
4. Lloyd, *History of Wales*, Vol. 2, p. 359.
5. Asser, *Life of King Alfred*, eds and trans. S. Keynes and M. Lapidge (Harmondsworth: Penguin Books, 1983), p. 96.
6. Ifor Williams (ed.), *Armes Prydein* (Cardiff: University of Wales Press, 1955).
7. Thomas Jones (ed. and trans.), *Brut y Tywysogyon (Peniarth MS 20 version)* (Cardiff: University of Wales Press, 1952) p. 16.
8. J. Gwenogvryn Evans and J. Rhys (ed), *The Text of the Book of Llan Dâv* (Oxford: 1893, reprinted Aberystwyth, National Library of Wales, 1979), p. 278.
9. *Domesday Book* (London, 1783), Vol. 1, p. 179a.
10. Ibid., p. 269a.
11. Evans, *Historia Gruffud vab Kenan*, p. 10.
12. Ibid., pp. 14–16.
13. Jones, *Brut y Tywysogyon (Peniarth MS 20 version)*, p. 19.
14. Ibid., pp. 27–8.
15. 'A treatise of Lordshipps Marchers in Wales' in Henry Owen (ed.), *The Description of Penbrokeshire by George Owen of Henllys Lord of Kemes*, Vol. 3 (London: Cymmrodorion Record Series, 1906), p. 139.
16. Edwards, 'The Normans and the Welsh march', pp. 163–77.
17. Davies, 'Kings, lords and liberties in the march of Wales', pp. 41–61.
18. A. H. A. Hogg and D. J. C. King, 'Early castles in Wales and the marches: a preliminary list', *Archaeologia Cambrensis*, 112 (1963), pp. 77–124.

141

19. William Rees, *Cardiff: a history of the city*, 2nd edn, (Cardiff Corporation, 1969), p. 54.
20. Rees, *South Wales and the March*, pp. 229–34.
21. M. Chibnall, *Anglo-Norman England 1066–1176* (Oxford: Basil Blackwell, 1986), p. 46.
22. Jones, *Brut y Tywysogyon (Peniarth 20 version)*, p. 38.
23. Ibid., p. 45.
24. Thomas Jones (ed. and trans.), *Brut y Tywysogyon (Red Book of Hergest version)* (Cardiff: University of Wales Press, 1955), p. 91.
25. Evans, *Historia Gruffud vab Kenan*, pp. 30–1.
26. Jones, *Brut y Tywysogyon (Peniarth 20 version)*, p. 68.
27. Michael Richter, 'The political and institutional background to national consciousness in medieval Wales', in T. W. Moody (ed.), *Nationality and the Pursuit of National Independence* (Belfast: Appletree Press, 1978), pp. 41–2.
28. D. M. Lloyd, 'The poets of the princes' in *Guide to Welsh Literature*, Vol. 1, p. 157–88.
29. Evans, *Historia Gruffud vab Kenan*, p. 30.
30. Jones, *Brut y Tywysogyon (Peniarth 20 version)*, pp. 35, 45–6.
31. Lewis, 'Treaty of Woodstock', pp. 63–4.
32. C. Bullock-Davies, *Professional Interpreters and the Matter of Britain* (Cardiff: University of Wales Press, 1966).
33. J. E. Caerwyn Williams, 'Aberteifi 1176', *Taliesin*, 32 (1976), pp. 33–5.
34. M. Lapidge, 'The Welsh Latin poetry of Sulien's family', *Studia Celtica*, 8–9 (1973–4), pp. 68–106.
35. H. E. Butler (ed. and trans.), *The Autobiography of Giraldus Cambrensis* (London: Jonathan Cape, 1937), p. 82.
36. The most recent discussion is Wendy Davies, 'The myth of the Celtic church' in Nancy Edwards and Alan Lane (eds), *The Early Church in Wales and the West* (Oxford: Oxbow monographs, 1992), pp. 12–21.
37. *Episcopal Acts*, Vol. 1, p. 249.
38. David H. Williams, *The Welsh Cistercians*, Vol. 1 2nd edn (Tenby: Cyhoeddiadau Sistersiaidd, 1984), pp. 1–21.
39. Lloyd, *History of Wales*, Vol. 2, p. 596.
40. Williams, *Welsh Church*, p. 18; these were Bardsey, Beddgelert and Penmon.
41. *Episcopal Acts*, Vol. 1, pp. 190–204; Richter, *Giraldus Cambrensis*, pp. 40–60.
42. Butler, *Autobiography of Giraldus Cambrensis*, pp. 129–350.
43. *Episcopal Acts*, Vol. 1, p. 210.

44. Gerald of Wales, *The Journey through Wales and the Description of Wales*, ed. and trans. Lewis Thorpe (Harmondsworth: Penguin Books, 1978).
45. Bartlett, *Gerald of Wales*, pp. 158–77.
46. Richter, *Giraldus Cambrensis*, pp. 81–2.

3. THE AGE OF THE PRINCES

1. Gwyn A. Williams, 'When was Wales?' in *The Welsh in their History* (London: Croom Helm, 1982), p. 192.
2. Wynn, *History of the Gwydir Family*, p. 3.
3. Gerald of Wales, *Journey*, pp. 193–4.
4. T. Rymer (ed.), *Foedera, Conventiones, Litterae etc.*, 4th edn (London: 1816–64), Vol. 1 (i), p. 84.
5. Lloyd, *History of Wales*, Vol. 2, p. 622.
6. J. Beverley Smith, 'Magna Carta and the charters of the Welsh princes', *EHR*, 99 (1984), pp. 361–2.
7. R. F. Treharne, 'The Franco-Welsh alliance of 1212', *BBCS*, 18 (1958), pp. 74–5.
8. W. Stubbs (ed.), *Select Charters and other illustrations of English constitutional history* (9th edn. rev. H. W. C. Davis (Oxford: Clarendon Press, 1913), p. 300.
9. Jones, *Brut y Tywysogyon (Peniarth 20 version)*, p. 92.
10. F. M. Powicke, *The Thirteenth Century* (Oxford: Clarendon Press, 1953), p. 386.
11. Rymer, *Foedera*, Vol. 1 (i), p. 150.
12. *Calendar of the Patent Rolls 1232–1247*, p. 59.
13. Richter, 'Political and institutional background', p. 43.
14. Lloyd, *History of Wales*, Vol. 2, p. 687.
15. Matthew Paris, *Chronica Majora*, ed. H. R. Luard Vol. 5 (London: Rolls Series, 1880), p. 718.
16. Edwards, *Littere Wallie*, pp. 5–6.
17. Ibid., pp. 9–10.
18. Ibid., pp. 10–12.
19. Michael Richter, 'David ap Llywelyn, the first prince of Wales', *WHR*, 5 (1971), pp. 208–13.
20. Ibid., pp. 205–10.
21. Lloyd, *History of Wales*, Vol. 2, p. 694.
22. Edwards, *Littere Wallie*, pp. 7–8.
23. Smith, *Llywelyn ap Gruffudd*, pp. 66–9.
24. Ibid., pp. 71–3.

25. Jones, *Brut y Tywysogyon (Peniarth 20 version)*, p. 111.
26. Edwards, *Littere Wallie*, pp. 184–6; Smith, *Llywelyn ap Gruffudd*, p. 98; this is Llywelyn's first surviving use of the title.
27. Edwards, *Littere Wallie*, pp. 77–80; Jones, *Brut y Tywysogyon* (Peniarth 20 version), p. 113.
28. *Foedera*, Vol. 1 (i), p. 457.
29. T. F. Tout, 'Wales and the march during the Barons' Wars', in *Collected Papers*, Vol. 2 (Manchester University Press, 1934) p. 54n., citing Dunstable Annals.
30. R. F. Treharne, *The Baronial Plan of Reform 1258–1263* (Manchester University Press, 1932), pp. 130–1, 194–5.
31. Edwards, *Littere Wallie*, pp. 1–4.
32. *Calendar of Chancery Rolls Various (Welsh Rolls)*, p. 199.
33. Davies, 'Survival of the bloodfeud', p. 355 and n.
34. D. Stephenson, *The Governance of Gwynedd* (Cardiff: University of Wales Press, 1984), pp. 5 and n.–6, 82–9; Davies, *Conquest, Coexistence and Change*, pp. 260–1.
35. This is illustrated in T. Matthews, *Welsh Records in Paris* (Carmarthen: Spurrell, 1910), facing p. 3.
36. Stephenson, *Governance of Gwynedd*, p. 26.
37. Edwards, *Littere Wallie*, pp. 74–5; P. Vinogradoff and F. Morgan (eds), *Survey of the Honour of Denbigh 1334* (London: British Academy, 1914), p. 297.
38. Jones, *Brut y Tywysogyon (Peniarth 20 version)*, p. 102; Williams ab Ithel, *Annales Cambriae*, p. 100.
39. Tout, 'Wales and the march during the Barons' Wars', p. 61.
40. G. R. J. Jones, 'The defences of Gwynedd in the thirteenth century', *TCHS*, 30 (1969), pp. 33–41.
41. R. Avent, *Cestyll Tywysogion Gwynedd/Castles of the Princes of Gwynedd* (Cardiff: HMSO, 1982), pp. 17–20.
42. Edwards, 'Edward I's castle-building', p. 15.
43. Jones Pierce, 'Growth of commutation' in *Medieval Welsh Society*, p. 120.
44. Una Rees (ed.), *The Cartulary of Haughmond Abbey* (Cardiff: University of Wales Press, 1985), no. 787 (p. 160a).
45. Rees, *Calendar of Ancient Petitions*, pp. 82–3.
46. T. Jones Pierce, 'Lleyn ministers' accounts, 1350–1', *BBCS*, 6 (1932), p. 265; 'Two early Caernarvonshire accounts', *BBCS*, 5 (1930), pp. 143–8.
47. J. G. Edwards (ed.), *Calendar of Ancient Correspondence concerning Wales*, (Cardiff: University of Wales Press, 1935), pp. 209–10.
48. Ibid., p. 86.

49. Edwards, *Littere Wallie*, pp. 136–8.
50. Jones, *Brut y Tywysogyon (Peniarth 20 version)*, p. 117.
51. J. E. Morris, *The Welsh Wars of King Edward the First* (Oxford: Clarendon Press, 1901), p. 115.
52. A. J. Taylor, *The Welsh Castles of Edward I* (London: Hambledon Press, 1986), pp. 1–37.
53. Edwards, *Littere Wallie*, pp. 118–22.
54. Ibid., p. lxi.
55. Williams-Jones, *Merioneth Lay Subsidy Roll*, pp. xvii–xx.
56. Ibid., p. cxxvi.
57. Smith, *Llywelyn ap Gruffudd*, pp. 329 and n.–330.
58. *Calendar of Chancery Rolls Various*, pp. 190–210.
59. *Calendar of Ancient Correspondence*, p. 76.
60. Morris, *Welsh Wars*, p. 153.
61. Ibid., pp. 154–5.
62. D. L. Douie, *Archbishop Pecham* (Oxford: Clarendon Press, 1952), pp. 235–53.
63. C. T. Martin (ed.), *Registrum Epistolarum Fratris Johannis Peckham, Archiepiscopi Cantuarensis* Vol. 2 (London: Rolls Series, 1884), pp. 440–65.
64. Ibid., pp. 435–7, 467–8.
65. Ibid., pp. 469–71; Davies, 'Law and national identity', p. 52.
66. Edwards, *Littere Wallie*, pp. 151, 154–7.
67. Smith, *Llywelyn ap Gruffudd*, pp. 344–5, 353–4.
68. A. J. Roderick, 'The conquest of Wales', in A. J. Roderick (ed.), *Wales through the Ages*, (Llandybie: Christopher Davies, 1959), p. 121.
69. Davies, *Welsh Assize Roll*, p. 266.
70. R. R. Davies, *Domination and Conquest: the experience of Ireland, Scotland and Wales 1100–1300* (Cambridge University Press, 1990), pp. 113–28.
71. Smith, *Llywelyn ap Gruffudd*, pp. 191–8.
72. Smith, '*Gravamina* of the community of Gwynedd', pp. 153–76.
73. Jones, *Brut y Tywysogyon (Peniarth 20 version)*, p. 120.
74. J. G. Edwards, 'Sir Gruffydd Llwyd', *EHR*, 30 (1915), p. 558n.
75. A. D. Carr, 'An aristocracy in decline: the native Welsh lords after the Edwardian conquest', *WHR*, 5 (1970), p. 111 and n.

4 SETTLEMENT AND CRISIS

1. Ivor Bowen, *The Statutes of Wales* (London: T. Fisher Unwin, 1908), pp. 2–27.

2. J. G. Edwards, 'The early history of the counties of Carmarthen and Cardigan', *EHR*, 31 (1916), pp. 90–8.
3. *Calendar of Ancient Correspondence*, p. 48.
4. Roberts, 'Wyrion Eden', pp. 40–55.
5. Griffiths, *Principality of Wales*, pp. 99–102.
6. Taylor, *Welsh Castles of Edward I*, pp. 45–126.
7. A. D. Carr, *Medieval Anglesey* (Llangefni: Anglesey Antiquarian Society, 1982), pp. 256–7.
8. Lewis, *Mediaeval Boroughs of Snowdonia*, especially pp. 21–98
9. M. Beresford, *New Towns of the Middle Ages: town plantation in England, Wales and Gascony*, 2nd edn (Gloucester: Alan Sutton, 1988).
10. Ralph A. Griffiths, 'The revolt of Rhys ap Maredudd, 1287–8' *WHR*, 3 (1966), pp. 121–43; J. Beverley Smith, 'The origins of the revolt of Rhys ap Maredudd', *BBCS*, 21 (1965), pp. 151–63.
11. J. Griffiths, 'The revolt of Madog ap Llywelyn, 1294–5', *TCHS*, 16 (1955), pp. 12–24; R. F. Walker, 'The Welsh war of 1294–5' in E. B. Fryde (ed.), *A Book of Prests of the King's Wardrobe for 1294–5 presented to John Goronwy Edwards* (Oxford: Clarendon Press, 1962), pp. xxvi–liii.
12. Carr, *Medieval Anglesey*, pp. 57–8.
13. Davies, *Conquest, Coexistence and Change*, p. 386.
14. M. Altschul, 'Glamorgan and Morgannwg under the rule of the de Clare family' in T. B. Pugh (ed.) *Glamorgan County History* Vol. 3 (Cardiff: University of Wales Press, 1971), pp. 57–9.
15. J. Beverley Smith, 'The rebellion of Llywelyn Bren' in *Glamorgan County History*, Vol. 3, pp. 72–86.
16. Smith, 'Gruffydd Llwyd and the Celtic alliance', pp. 463–78; Bowen, *Statutes of Wales*, pp. 27–9.
17. J. Conway Davies, 'The Despenser war in Glamorgan', *TRHS*, 3rd series, 9 (1915), p. 21–64.
18. Smith, 'Edward II and the allegiance of Wales', pp. 159–71.
19. D. L. Evans, 'Walter de Mauny, sheriff of Merioneth, 1322–72' *JMHRS* 4 (1963), pp. 196–9.
20. Bowen, *Statutes of Wales*, p. 30.
21. Roberts, 'Wyrion Eden', pp. 47–50.
22. D. L. Evans (ed.), *Flintshire Ministers' Accounts 1328–1353* (Flintshire Historical Society Record Series, 1929), pp. xxi–xxxix.
23. A. D. Carr, 'Welshmen and the Hundred Years War', *WHR*, 4 (1968) pp. 24, 27.
24. Wynn, *History of the Gwydir Family*, p. 17.
25. Carr, 'Welshmen and the Hundred Years War', pp. 26–7.

26. R. R. Davies, *Lordship and Society in the March of Wales* 1282–1400 (Oxford: Clarendon Press, 1978), p. 360.

27. Llinos Beverley Smith, 'The gage and the land market in late medieval Wales', *EconHR*, 2nd series, 29 (1976), pp. 537–50; '*Tir prid*: deeds of gage of land in late medieval Wales', *BBCS*, 27 (1977), pp. 263–77.

28. A. D. Carr, 'The making of the Mostyns: the genesis of a landed family', *THSC* 1979, pp. 152–6; 'Gwilym ap Gruffydd and the rise of the Penrhyn estate', *WHR*, 15 (1990), pp. 1–5.

29. Davies, *Lordship and Society*, pp. 224–5; C. R. Williams, *The History of Flintshire* (Denbigh: Gee & Son, 1961), pp. 99–100.

30. J. H. Matthews (ed.), *Records of the County Borough of Cardiff*, Vol. 1 (Cardiff Corporation, 1898), pp. 56–7, 58.

31. Rachel Bromwich, 'Dafydd ap Gwilym', 'The earlier *cywyddwyr*: poets contemporary with Dafydd ap Gwilym' in A. O. H. Jarman and G. R. Hughes (eds), *A Guide to Welsh Literature* Vol. 2 (Swansea: Christopher Davies, 1979), pp. 112–68.

32. Morfydd E. Owen, 'The prose of the *cywydd* period', in *Guide to Welsh Literature*, Vol. 2, pp. 338–75.

33. Stephen J. Williams (ed.), *Ffordd y Brawd Odrig* (Cardiff: University of Wales Press, 1929).

34. Carr, *Medieval Anglesey*, pp. 143–50.

35. T. Jones Pierce, 'Medieval settlement in Anglesey', in *Medieval Welsh Society*, pp. 274–6.

36. J. W. Willis-Bund (ed.), *The Black Book of St David's 1326* (London: Cymmrodorion Record Series, 1902); Vinogradoff and Morgan, *Survey of the Honour of Denbigh 1334*; Ellis, *Record of Caernarvon*, pp. 1–89; British Library, Additional MS 10013.

37. R. R. Davies, 'Race relations in post-conquest Wales: confrontation and compromise', *THSC* (1974), pp. 32–56.

38. R. R. Davies, 'The status of women and the practice of marriage in late medieval Wales', in Dafydd Jenkins and Morfydd E. Owen (eds), *The Welsh Law of Women: studies presented to Professor Daniel A. Binchy on his eightieth birthday* (Cardiff: University of Wales Press, 1980), pp. 93–114; Carr, *Medieval Anglesey*, pp. 155–61.

39. Davies, 'Status of women', p. 107n.; Carr, *Medieval Anglesey*, pp. 180–1.

40. Williams-Jones, *Merioneth Lay Subsidy Roll*, p. xxxviii.

41. Davies, *Lordship and Society*, p. 447; Ralph A. Griffiths, 'Carmarthen', in *Boroughs of Medieval Wales*, pp. 160–1.

42. Lewis, *Mediaeval Boroughs of Snowdonia*, p. 196; Williams-Jones, *Merioneth Lay Subsidy Roll*, pp. lxi–lxii; A. D. Carr, 'The

chamberlain's account and the county of Flint', in P. H. W. Booth and A, D. Carr (eds), *Account of Master John de Burnham the younger, Chamberlain of Chester, of the revenues of the counties of Chester and Flint, Michaelmas 1361 to Michaelmas 1362* (Record Society of Lancashire and Cheshire 125, 1991), p. lxx.

43. Hallam, *Agrarian History of England and Wales*, Vol. 2, pp. 422–32.
44. Carr, *Medieval Anglesey*, p. 120; Henry Owen (ed.), *A Calendar of the Public Records relating to Pembrokeshire*, Vol. 3, (London: Cymmrodorion Record Series, 1918), p. 119.
45. Davies, *Lordship and Society*, p. 116.
46. Williams, *The Welsh Cistercians*, Vol. 2, p. 305.
47. Rees, *South Wales and the March*, p. 257; R. Ian Jack, 'The cloth industry in medieval Wales', *WHR*, 10 (1981), pp. 457–8; Davies, *Lordship and Society*, p. 118.
48. Jack, 'Cloth industry', pp. 443–54.
49. W. Linnard, *Welsh Woods and Forests: history and utilization* (Cardiff: National Museum of Wales, 1982), pp. 30–44.
50. Williams, *The Welsh Cistercians*, Vol. 2, p. 327.
51. Carr, 'Chamberlain's account and the county of Flint', pp. lxxviii–lxix; Rees, *Industry before the Industrial Revolution*, Vol. 1, pp. 34–5.
52. Williams, *The Welsh Cistercians*, Vol. 2, pp. 326–9; Rees, *Industry before the Industrial Revolution*, Vol. 1, pp. 36–42.
53. Lewis, 'A contribution to the commercial history of medieval Wales', p. 115.
54. A. Jones (ed.), *Flintshire Ministers' Accounts 1301–1328* (Flintshire Historical Society, 1913), pp. xliii–xlv.
55. H. E. Hallam, *Rural England 1066–1348* (London: Fontana, 1981), p. 238.
56. Carr, *Medieval Anglesey*, p. 262; Ralph A. Griffiths, 'The boroughs of the lordship of Glamorgan' in *Glamorgan County History*, Vol. 3, p. 354.
57. Rees, 'The Black Death in Wales', pp. 181–5.
58. Ibid., pp. 185–6.
59. Ibid., pp. 186–7; Tomos Roberts, 'Englynion Gwynedd gan Gruffudd ap Maredudd ap Dafydd', *TAAS* (1982), pp. 123–7.
60. Lewis, 'Decay of tribalism', p. 45; Brown Willis, *A Survey of the Cathedral Church of St Asaph* (London, 1720), p. 241.
61. Davies, *Lordship and Society*, pp. 138–9.
62. A. D. Carr, 'The Welsh worker in the fourteenth century: an introduction to labour prehistory', *Llafur*, 5 (1988), p. 11; Davies, *Lordship and Society*, p. 247.
63. R. R. Davies, 'The lordship of Ogmore', in *Glamorgan County History*, Vol. 3, p. 299.

64. Carr, *Medieval Anglesey*, pp. 327–9.
65. *Calendar of Public Records relating to Pembrokeshire*, Vol. 3, p. 142.
66. A. R. Bridbury, 'The Black Death', *EconHR*, 2nd series, 26 (1973), p. 591.
67. A. D. Carr, *Owen of Wales: the end of the house of Gwynedd* (Cardiff: University of Wales Press, 1991) and references cited therein.
68. T. Jones Pierce, 'The social scene in the fourteenth century' in *Wales through the Ages*, Vol. 1, pp. 155–6.
69. Carr, *Owen of Wales*, pp. 89–91.
70. Gomer M. Roberts, *Hanes Plwyf Llandybie* (Cardiff: University of Wales Press, 1939), pp. 249–59.
71. Carr, 'The making of the Mostyns', pp. 144–5; T. D. Lloyd (ed.), *Baronia de Kemeys* (London: Cambrian Archaeological Association, 1861), pp. 125–33.
72. Glanmor Williams, *The Welsh Church from Conquest to Reformation*, 1st edn (Cardiff: University of Wales Press, 1962), pp. 122–39.

5. REBELLION AND REVENGE

1. Davies, *Conquest, Coexistence and Change*, p. 448.
2. D. R. Johnston (ed.), *Gwaith Iolo Goch* (Cardiff: University of Wales Press, 1988), pp. 46–8; for an English translation see A. Conran, *The Penguin Book of Welsh Verse* (Harmondsworth, Penguin Books, 1967), pp. 153–6.
3. A. Goodman, 'Owain Glyndŵr before 1400', *WHR*, 5 (1970), pp. 67–70.
4. Davies, 'Owain Glyn Dŵr and the Welsh squirearchy', pp. 154–64.
5. Johnston, *Gwaith Iolo Goch*, pp. 36–8; H. Lewis, T. Roberts, I. Williams (eds), *Cywyddau Iolo Goch ac Eraill*, 2nd edn (Cardiff: University of Wales Press, 1937), pp. 125–7.
6. J. E. Lloyd, *Owen Glendower* (Oxford: Clarendon Press, 1931), pp. 46–7, 68–9.
7. Owen, 'Owain Lawgoch – Yeuain de Galles', pp. 16–17n.
8. R.-H.Bautier, *The Economic Development of Medieval Europe*, trans. H. Karolyi (London: Thames & Hudson, 1971), pp. 231–2.
9. Lloyd, *Owen Glendower*, pp. 29–30.
10. Bowen, *Statutes of Wales*, pp. 31–4.
11. Ellis, *Record of Caernarvon*, pp. 131–2.
12. Williams-Jones, 'The taking of Conwy castle', esp. pp. 7–22.
13. Bowen, *Statutes of Wales*, pp. 34–6.
14. Ralph A. Griffiths, 'The Glyndŵr rebellion in north Wales through the eyes of an Englishman', *BBCS*, 22 (1967), pp. 155–8.

Notes and References

15. Williams, *The Welsh Church*, pp. 219–22.
16. Matthews, *Welsh Records in Paris*, pp. 25–31.
17. Ibid., pp. 108–10.
18. Ibid., pp. 42–54.
19. J. R. S. Phillips, 'When did Owain Glyndŵr die?', *BBCS*, 24 (1970), pp. 54–77.
20. Davies, *Conquest, Coexistence and Change*, p. 462.
21. J. Beverley Smith, 'The last phase of the Glyndŵr rebellion', *BBCS*, 22 (1967), pp. 254–6.
22. Griffiths, 'The Glyndŵr rebellion in north Wales', pp. 151–68.
23. Davies, *Conquest, Coexistence and Change*, pp. 458–9 and n.; Griffiths, *Principality of Wales*, pp. 139–41.
24. *Dictionary of Welsh Biography* (London: Honourable Society of Cymmrodorion, 1959), pp. 359–60; A. D. Carr, 'Sir Lewis John: a medieval London Welshman', *BBCS*, 22 (1967), pp. 260–70; H. T. Evans, *Wales and the Wars of the Roses* (Cambridge University Press, 1915), pp. 19–22.
25. Carr, 'Gwilym ap Gruffydd', pp. 10–11.
26. Griffiths, 'Carmarthen', pp. 154–5; Rees, *Cardiff; a history of the city*, p. 14; Williams-Jones, 'The taking of Conwy castle', pp. 22–3.
27. Gwyn A. Williams, 'Owain Glyn Dŵr', in *Wales through the Ages*, Vol. 1, p. 183.
28. Griffiths, 'Patronage, politics and the principality of Wales', pp. 70–84.
29. Ralph A. Griffiths, 'Gruffydd ap Nicholas and the rise of the house of Dinefwr', *NLWJ*, 13 (1964), pp. 257–65.
30. Griffiths, *Principality of Wales*, pp. 147–8; 'Patronage, politics and the principality of Wales', pp. 83–4.
31. Griffiths, 'Gentlemen and rebels', pp. 158–9; 'Gruffydd ap Nicholas and the fall of the house of Lancaster', *WHR*, 2 (1965), pp. 213–31.
32. Wynn, *History of the Gwydir Family*, pp. 28–54.
33. Griffiths, 'Wales and the marches', p. 155; Wynn, *History of the Gwydir Family*, pp. 51–7.
34. T. B. Pugh (ed.), *The Marcher Lordships of South Wales 1415–1536* (Cardiff: University of Wales Press, 1963), pp. 36, 31.
35. Griffiths, *Principality of Wales*, pp. 28–9.
36. J. Beverley Smith, 'The regulation of the frontier of Meirionnydd in the fifteenth century', *JMHRS*, 5 (1966), pp. 105–11; 'Cydfodau o'r bymthegfed ganrif', *BBCS*, 21 (1966), pp. 309–24.
37. Carr, 'Gwilym ap Gruffydd', pp. 17–20.
38. Ibid., pp. 7, 12–13.

150

39. Carr, *Medieval Anglesey*, p. 210.
40. Ibid., pp. 217–21; D. C. Jones, 'The Bulkeleys of Beaumaris, 1440–1547', *TAAS* 1961, pp. 1–20.
41. Carr, 'The making of the Mostyns', pp. 138–9.
42. Ralph A. Griffiths, *Sir Rhys ap Thomas and his Family* (Cardiff: University of Wales Press, 1993), pp. 27–86.
43. Ralph A. Griffiths, 'Richard, duke of York and the royal household in Wales, 1449–50', *WHR*, 8 (1976), p. 15–19.
44. Evans, *Wales and the Wars of the Roses*, pp. 102–7.
45. E. D. Jones (ed.), *Gwaith Lewis Glyn Cothi* (Cardiff: University of Wales Press and Aberystwyth, National Library of Wales, 1953), p. 4.
46. I. Williams and J. Llywelyn Williams (eds) *Gwaith Guto'r Glyn* 2nd edn (Cardiff: University of Wales Press, 1961) pp. 129–31.
47. Griffiths, *Principality of Wales*, pp. 187–8.
48. Saunders Lewis, 'Gyrfa filwrol Guto'r Glyn', in J. E. Caerwyn Williams (ed.), *Ysgrifau Beirniadol*, IX (Denbigh: Gwasg Gee, 1976), pp. 80–99.
49. Ralph A. Griffiths and Roger S. Thomas, *The Making of the Tudor Dynasty* (Gloucester: Alan Sutton, 1985), pp. 75–7.
50. W. Leslie Richards (ed.), *Gwaith Dafydd Llwyd o Fathafarn* (Cardiff: University of Wales Press, 1964), pp. 32, 49, 51, 94.
51. G. Aled Williams, 'The bardic road to Bosworth: a Welsh view of Henry Tudor', *THCS*, 1986, pp. 19–27.
52. Wynn, *History of the Gwydir Family*, p. 27.
53. Griffiths and Thomas, *Making of the Tudor Dynasty*, pp. 133–48.
54. Carr, *Medieval Anglesey*, pp. 229–30.
55. Glanmor Williams, *Recovery, Reorientation and Reformation: Wales c. 1415–1642* (Oxford: Clarendon Press, 1987), pp. 231–2.
56. 'The dialogue of the government of Wales', in Owen, *Description of Penbrokeshire*, Vol. 3, p. 37.
57. Williams, *Recovery, Reorientation and Reformation*, p. 241.
58. Ibid., pp. 235–7, 240–1.
59. Ibid., pp. 228–9, 243.
60. Smith, 'Crown and community', pp. 160–6.
61. Ibid., pp. 166–7.
62. C. Rawcliffe, *The Staffords, Earls of Stafford and Dukes of Buckingham* (Cambridge University Press, 1978), p. 128.
63. Smith, 'Crown and community', pp. 156–8.
64. Ibid., pp. 157–9; *CPR 1494–1509*, pp. 534–5.
65. *CPR 1494–1509*, pp. 434 (Bromfield and Yale), 464–5 (Chirk), 471 (Denbigh), 586–7 (Dyffryn Clwyd).

66. Smith, 'Crown and community', pp. 170–1.
67. Jarman and Hughes, *Guide to Welsh Literature*, Vol. 2, pp. 189–337.
68. Williams, *The Welsh Church*, pp. 428–33.
69. Ibid., pp. 387–402.
70. Ibid., pp. 488–97.
71. G. E. Ruddock, 'Siôn Cent', in Jarman and Hughes, *Guide to Welsh Literature*, Vol. 2, pp. 169–88.
72. Williams, *Recovery, Reorientation and Reformation*, p. 248.
73. W. R. B. Robinson, 'Early Tudor policy towards Wales: the acquisition of lands and offices in Wales by Charles Somerset, earl of Worcester', *BBCS*, 20 (1964), pp. 422–7.

CONCLUSION

1. G. N. Garmonsway (ed. and trans.), *The Anglo-Saxon Chronicle* (London, Everyman's Library, 1954), p. 191.
2. *Calendar of Chancery Warrants 1244–1326*, p. 76.
3. Carr, *Owen of Wales*, p. 67.

SELECT BIBLIOGRAPHY

This bibliography is intended to provide no more than an introduction to the books and articles which deal with the history of medieval Wales. In addition to the works listed here, many are cited in the references to each chapter. Those seeking further reading will find excellent bibliographies in R. R. Davies, *Conquest, Coexistence and Change: Wales 1063–1415*, and Glanmor Williams, *Recovery, Reorientation and Reformation: Wales c. 1415–1642*; the most exhaustive bibliography is the revised *Bibliography of the History of Wales*, ed. P. H. Jones (Cardiff: University of Wales Press, 1990: available only on microfiche).

The Agrarian History of England and Wales, Vol. 2, 1042–1348, H. E. Hallam (ed.); *Vol. 3, 1348–1500*, E. Miller (ed.) (Cambridge University Press, 1988, 1991) – Wales is well-covered in both volumes.

Avent, R., *Cestyll Tywysogion Gwynedd/Castles of the Princes of Gwynedd* (Cardiff: HMSO, 1983) – the native Welsh castles.

Carr, A. D., 'Welshmen and the Hundred Years War', *Welsh History Review*, 4 (1968), pp. 21–46 – describes Welsh involvement in the war.

——, *Medieval Anglesey* (Llangefni: Anglesey Antiquarian Society, 1982) – a detailed local study.

——, *Owen of Wales: the end of the house of Gwynedd* (Cardiff: University of Wales Press, 1991) – examines the French dimension in fourteenth-century Welsh politics and contemporary social and political tensions.

Davies, R. R., 'The twilight of Welsh law, 1284–1536', *History* 51 (1966), pp. 143–64 – surveys the use of Welsh law between the Statute of Wales and the first Act of Union.

——, 'Owain Glyn Dŵr and the Welsh squirearchy', *Transactions of the Honourable Society of Cymmrodorion*, 1968, (ii), pp. 150–69 – outlines the network of family connections among the leaders of the native community and its significance in the revolt.

——, 'Race relations in post-conquest Wales', *Transactions of the Honourable Society of Cymmrodorion* (1974–5), pp. 32–56 – examines the relations of native Welsh and English immigrants, especially in the northern march.

——, *Lordship and Society in the March of Wales 1282–1400* (Oxford; Clarendon Press, 1978) – a detailed discussion of the nature of marcher lordship and society.

——, 'Kings, lords and liberties in the march of Wales, 1066–1272', *Transactions of the Royal Historical Society*, 5th series, 29 (1979), pp. 41–61 – the most recent discussion of the nature of marcher lordship.

——, 'Law and national identity in thirteenth-century Wales' in R. R. Davies *et al.*, (eds), *Welsh Society and Nationhood: essays presented to Glanmor Williams* (Cardiff: University of Wales Press, 1984), pp. 51–69 – considers the emergence of a sense of national identity during the thirteenth century.

——, *Conquest, Coexistence and Change: Wales 1066–1415* (Oxford: Clarendon Press, 1987) – now the standard work on the period.

——, *Domination and Conquest: the experience of Ireland, Scotland and Wales 1100–1300* (Cambridge University Press, 1990) – examines the development of the relationship of the English crown with the other nations of the British Isles.

Davies, Wendy, *Wales in the Early Middle Ages* (Leicester University Press, 1982) – now the standard work on pre-Norman Wales.

Edwards, J. G., *Littere Wallie preserved in Liber A in the Public Record Office* (Cardiff: University of Wales Press, 1940) – the first discussion of the events leading up to the conquest and the starting-point of subsequent debate.

——, 'The Normans and the Welsh march', *Proceedings of the British Academy*, 42 (1956), pp. 155–77 – the first revisionist discussion of marcher lordship.

Evans, H. T., *Wales and the Wars of the Roses* (Cambridge University Press, 1915) – an early work which is still useful.

Griffiths, Ralph A., *The Principality of Wales in the Later Middle Ages: the structure and personnel of government, I: South Wales 1277–1536* (Cardiff: University of Wales Press, 1972) – a prosopography with a valuable introduction.

——, 'Wales and the marches' in S. B. Chrimes, C. D. Ross and R. A. Griffiths (eds), *Fifteenth-century England 1399–1509* (Manchester

University Press, 1972) – an overview of fifteenth-century Welsh politics.

——, *Boroughs of Medieval Wales* (Cardiff, University of Wales Press, 1978) – a number of studies of individual towns by different authors.

——, *Sir Rhys ap Thomas and his Family: a study in the Wars of the Roses and early Tudor politics* (Cardiff: University of Wales Press, 1993) – examines Sir Rhys ap Thomas and his family background and includes the first scholarly edition of a seventeenth-century biography.

Jack, R. Ian, *Medieval Wales* (London: Hodder & Stoughton, 1972) – examines the sources available for the study of medieval Wales.

Jarman, A. O. H. and Hughes, G. R. (eds), *A Guide to Welsh Literature* 2 vols (Swansea: Christopher Davies, 1976, 1979) – a collection of studies which is the best introduction in English to medieval Welsh literature.

Jenkins, Dafydd, *The Law of Hywel Dda* (Llandysul: Gomer Press, 1986) – a composite text in translation.

Jones, G. R. J., 'The defences of Gwynedd in the thirteenth century', *Transactions of the Caernarvonshire Historical Society*, 30 (1969), pp. 29–43 – discusses the defensive and military policies of the native princes.

Jones, Thomas (ed. and trans.), *Brut y Tywysogyon: the Chronicle of the Princes: Peniarth MS 20 version*; *Red Book of Hergest version*; *Brenhinedd y Saesson or the Kings of the Saxons* (Cardiff: University of Wales Press, 1952, 1955, 1971) – the main Welsh chronicle down to 1282.

Jones Pierce, T., *Medieval Welsh Society* (Cardiff: University of Wales Press, 1972) – the most important articles by one of the most perceptive and original students of medieval Wales.

Lewis, E. A., 'The decay of tribalism in north Wales', *Transactions of the Honourable Society of Cymmrodorion*, (1902–3) – the first archive-based study of post-conquest Wales.

——, *The Mediaeval Boroughs of Snowdonia* (London: Henry Sotheran, for the University of Wales, 1912) – a pioneering study in Welsh urban history.

Lloyd, J. E., *A History of Wales from the earliest times to the Edwardian Conquest*, 2 vols, 1st edn (London: Longman, 1911) – the first history of Wales by a professional historian and a seminal work, as well as still being the basic narrative account.

——, *Owen Glendower* (Oxford: Clarendon Press, 1931) – remains the basic narrative account of the revolt.

Messham, J. E., 'The county of Flint and the rebellion of Owen Glyndwr in the records of the earldom of Chester', *Journal of the Flintshire Historical Society*, 23 (1967–8), pp. 1–34 – a model local study of the course and impact of the revolt.

Morris, J. E., *The Welsh Wars of King Edward the First* (Oxford: Clarendon Press, 1901) – the only detailed account of these wars, although amended and corrected by later research.

Nelson, Lynn H., *The Normans in South Wales, 1071–1170* (Austin: University of Texas Press, 1966) – an attempt, not entirely successful, to apply the Turner frontier thesis to the Welsh march, but containing much perceptive comment.

Powel, David, *The Historie of Cambria, now called Wales* (London: 1588) – the principal source for the history of medieval Wales before J. E. Lloyd.

Pugh, T. B. (ed.), *Glamorgan County History*, Vol. 3, (Cardiff: University of Wales Press, 1971) – a detailed study of the largest marcher lordship.

Rees, William, 'The Black Death in Wales', *Transactions of the Royal Historical Society*, 4th series, 3 (1920), pp. 115–35; reprinted in R. W. Southern (ed.), *Essays in Medieval History* (London: Macmillan, 1968), pp. 179–99 – still the only general study of the impact of the plague on Wales.

——, *South Wales and the March 1284–1415: a social and agrarian study* (Oxford University Press, 1924) – a pioneering work, based on detailed archival research.

Richter, Michael, 'David ap Llywelyn, the first prince of Wales', *Welsh History Review*, 5 (1971), pp. 205–19 – examines the reign of a prince often overshadowed by the two Llywelyns.

——, *Giraldus Cambrensis: the growth of the Welsh nation* 2nd edn (Aberystwyth: National Library of Wales, 1972) – discusses the Welsh dimension of Gerald's career.

——, 'The political and institutional background to national consciousness in medieval Wales' in T. W. Moody (ed.), *Nationality and the Pursuit of National Independence* (Belfast; Appletree Press, 1978), pp. 37–55 – discusses the development of native political authority, especially in the late twelfth century.

Roberts, Glyn *Aspects of Welsh History* (Cardiff: University of Wales Press, 1969) – collected papers, including two pioneering studies of the pre-1485 history of the Tudor lineage.

Smith, J. Beverley, 'Crown and community in the principality of north Wales in the reign of Henry Tudor', *Welsh History Review*, 3 (1966), pp. 145–71 – a wide-ranging discussion of the relationship of government and community, especially its financial aspects.

——, 'Edward II and the allegiance of Wales', *Welsh History Review*, 8 (1976), pp. 139–71 – examines Welsh attitudes and responses to the events and problems of Edward's reign.

——, *Llywelyn ap Gruffudd, Tywysog Cymru* (Cardiff: University of Wales Press, 1986) – the standard work on Llywelyn ap Gruffydd; an English version is in preparation.

Smith, Llinos Beverley, 'The gage and the land market in late medieval Wales', *Economic History Review*, 2nd series, 29 (1976), pp. 537–50 – examines the development and use of the Welsh *tir prid* conveyance in the late medieval land market.

——, 'The Statute of Wales, 1284', *Welsh History Review*, 10 (1980), pp. 127–54 – the legal context of the Statute.

——, 'The death of Llywelyn ap Gruffydd: the narratives re-considered', *Welsh History Review* 11 (1982), pp. 200–13 – what actually happened in December 1282.

Stephenson, David, *The Governance of Gwynedd* (Cardiff: University of Wales Press, 1984) – examines the administrative and institutional structure of the pre-conquest principality.

Taylor, A. J., *The Welsh Castles of Edward I*, 2nd edn (London: Hambledon Press, 1986) – a detailed account of the planning and construction of the Edwardian castles.

Walker, David, *The Norman Conquerors* (Swansea: Christopher Davies, 1977) – the Norman impact on Wales.

——, *Medieval Wales* (Cambridge University Press, 1990) – a useful general survey.

Williams, David H., *The Welsh Cistercians*, 2 vols, 2nd edn (Tenby: Cyhoeddiadau Sistersiaidd, 1984) – a detailed study of the order in medieval Wales.

Williams, Glanmor, *The Welsh Church from Conquest to Reformation* 2nd edn (Cardiff: University of Wales Press, 1976) – the point of departure for any work on the late medieval church.

——, *Recovery, Reorientation and Reformation: Wales, c. 1415–1642* (Oxford, Clarendon Press, 1987) – now the standard work on this period.

Williams-Jones, Keith, *The Merioneth Lay Subsidy Roll 1292–3* (Cardiff: University of Wales Press, 1976) – examines the social and economic background in Gwynedd before and after the conquest.

INDEX

158

Index

Philip II (Augustus), king of
France 56, 68
Pierce, T. Jones 17–18, 19, 20–1
Pipton, Treaty of, 1265 64–5
plague 100–3, 105, 110, 117
Plantagenet, Richard, duke of
York 121, 122, 129
poetry 10, 46, 93–4, 106, 109, 111,
125, 127, 130
poets 10, 46, 48, 93–4, 109, 123, 125,
126, 127, 131
Powel, David 8–10, 11
Powicke, Sir Maurice 25, 57
Powys 5, 6, 25, 27, 35, 40, 41, 42, 46,
54, 55–6, 57, 58, 63, 71, 76, 77,
78, 87, 89, 100, 103, 108–9, 110,
113, 115, 133
Price, Thomas (Carnhuanawc) 11
prophecy 8, 106, 109–10, 125
Pwllheli (Caerns.) 17, 70–1, 86, 96,
98

Radnor 35
Raglan (Mon.) 119, 123, 125, 126,
130
Ranulf III, earl of Chester 69
Rees, William 16–17
Reformation 7–8, 132
Renaissance 7, 8, 132
Rhodri ap Gruffydd 62
Rhodri ab Owain Gwynedd 55
Rhodri Mawr 27
Rhos (Denbs.) 42
Rhuddlan (Flints.) 32, 74, 78, 83, 86
Rhuddlan, Robert of 32–3, 35, 40
Rhydodyn (Carms.) 121
Rhygyfarch ap Sulien 48
Rhys ap Gruffydd (the Lord Rhys),
prince of Deheubarth 42, 43,
44, 45–6, 48–9, 54–5, 58
Rhys ap Gruffydd, Sir 84
Rhys ap Maredudd 87
Rhys ab Owain, king of
Deheubarth 33
Rhys ap Tewdwr, king of
Deheubarth 32, 33, 34, 44, 47,
48
Rhys ap Thomas, Sir 121, 126, 127,
131
Rhys ap Tudur ap Goronwy 112

Richard I, king of England 46
Richard II, king of England 109,
111–12
Richard III, king of England 123,
125–6
Richmond, earl of see Tudor,
Edmund; Tudor, Henry
Roberts, Glyn 18, 19
Rome 4, 7, 8, 51, 52, 61, 131
Roses, Wars of the 85, 122–3
Ruthin (Denbs.) 74, 96, 100, 112,
130

St Asaph 117
St Asaph, bishop of 101 (see also
Anian II; Trefor, John)
St David's 5, 7, 32, 44, 49, 51–3, 95,
115, 131
St David's, bishop of, see Bernard;
Davies, Richard; Fitz Gerald,
David
St George, Master James of 85
Sais, Sir Gregory 92, 109
Scotland 28, 31, 56, 63, 80–1, 89,
109, 113
Scudamore, Sir John 116
Sempringham (Lincs.) 79
Severn, river 34, 76
sheep 50, 93, 97, 130
Shrewsbury 30, 32, 34, 35, 79, 99,
126
Shrewsbury, battle of, 1403 113
Shrewsbury, earls of see Bellême,
Robert of; Hugh; Montgomery,
Roger of
Siôn Cent, poet 131
Smith, J. Beverley 21, 25–6
Smith, Llinos Beverley 21
Snowdonia 27, 69, 70, 74, 78, 79
Somerset, Charles, earl of
Worcester 131
Stafford, Edward, duke of
Buckingham 129, 131–2, 133
Stafford, Henry, duke of
Buckingham 125
Stanley, Thomas, Lord 126
Stanley, Sir William 126, 127–8
Stephen, king of England 42
Stephenson, David 21
Stradling, Sir Edward 9–10